Mel Cheatham has given us a hard-to-put-down-book telling of his struggles and success in becoming an outstanding neurosurgeon. Whether in terms of years or days, the matter of what you will do with the rest of your life will not turn you loose.

—**Billy and Ruth Graham**

Perhaps no question lingers with us as much, yet is ignored by us more than the question, "What am I going to do with the rest of my life?" In *Living a Life That Counts*, Mel Cheatham shares how this question prompted him to move beyond professional success as a respected neurosurgeon to a distinctive life of service. You will be uplifted, inspired, challenged, and led to live your own life in such a way that it will truly count.

—**Dr. Robert H. Schuller**
Founding Pastor, The Crystal Cathedral

Forget all those self-help books and read *Living a Life That Counts*. In this heart-searching book, Dr. Mel Cheatham, one of the world's leading neurosurgeons, reveals the underpinnings of his own exceptional life and relates how the biblical insights that transformed him can impact you and me.

—**Franklin Graham**
President, Samaritan's Purse

Dealing with the question, "What am I going to do with the rest of my life?" leads one to the even greater question, "What is it *God* wants me to do with the rest of my life?" No matter what your age, this book will speak to your heart.

—**Ricky Skaggs**
Country music artist

Inspiring, convicting, encouraging . . . this is a book that puts hands and feet to the call of God to be true servants. The many examples of people who are abandoned to the will of God serve to prove that true living begins with complete surrender to Him. Most impressive is the fact that Mel Cheatham lives the principles of this book. You will be challenged to do the same.

—**Michael W. and Debbie Smith**
Recording artist and wife

This is a book for everyone to read because, sooner or later, each of us comes to the place of reevaluating our objectives, goals, and dreams. The unforgettable stories of people who did just this—their stories alone—make Mel Cheatham's book a must.

—June Allyson
Actress of stage and screen

Dr. Melvin Cheatham in his remarkable book, *Living a Life That Counts*, writes with candor about his youthful years as a physician when "underneath the doctor's coat was a man who didn't know why he felt so empty when his career seemed so full." His honesty and humanity as he recounts his journey toward self-discovery and faith will intrigue you and ultimately draw you in. And the people Dr. Cheatham meets along the way will inspire you and remain in your mind for a long time. *Living a Life That Counts* is a book that counts!

—David and Julie Eisenhower

I have never read such moving accounts of men and women who have given so much to meet the needs of those who have so little, often in circumstances of extremely high risk. Of great significance is the fact that in the process, thousands have come to Christ. No one can read this book without becoming a better person.

—C. Davis Weyerhaeuser
President, Stewardship Foundation

LIVING A LIFE THAT COUNTS

MELVIN CHEATHAM, M.D.

WITH MARK CUTSHALL

THOMAS NELSON PUBLISHERS
Nashville • Atlanta • London • Vancouver

Published in Nashville, Tennessee, by Thomas Nelson, Inc., Publishers, and distributed in Canada by Word Communications, Ltd., Richmond, British Columbia, and in the United Kingdom by Word (UK), Ltd., Milton Keynes, England.

Unless otherwise noted, all Scripture quotations are from the NEW KING JAMES VERSION of the Bible, © 1979, 1980, 1982 by Thomas Nelson, Inc., Publishers.

Scriptures noted NIV are from The Holy Bible: NEW INTERNATIONAL VERSION. Copyright © 1978 by the New York International Bible Society. Used by permission of Zondervan Bible Publishers.

Library of Congress Cataloging-in-Publication Data

Cheatham, Melvin L.
    Living a life that counts / Melvin L. Cheatham with Mark Cutshall.
        p.   cm.
    Includes bibliographical references.
    ISBN 0-7852-7724-2
    1. Cheatham, Melvin L. 2. Neurosurgeons—United States—Biography.
3. Service (Theology) 4. Vocation. 5. Christian biography. I. Cutshall,
Mark. II. Title.
RD592.9.C47A3 1995
617.4'8092—dc20
[B]   95-10899
                                                                          CIP

Printed in the United States of America

1 2 3 4 5 6 7 — 01 00 99 98 97 96 95

This book is dedicated to my family, who has made the walk with me in trying to *Live a Life That Counts.* It is also dedicated to our extended family around the world, fellow workers who give of themselves in bringing help, hope, and God's love to those whom others have passed by.

CONTENTS

Foreword

Mel Cheatham has given us a hard-to-put-down book telling of his struggles and success in becoming an outstanding neurosurgeon. Into this story he weaves those of people who have asked and for whom God has answered the question, "What am I going to do with the rest of my life?"

The stories are not only gripping, but the very question will not leave you alone. Whether in terms of years or days, the matter of what you will do with the rest of your life will not turn you loose.

We know you will enjoy this book as we have and that you will be challenged by it.

—Billy and Ruth Graham

Acknowledgments

One of the most sought-after goals is a life worthy of recognition. People want to be noticed. They want to rise above the crowd and do that which will be distinctive. Many seek to achieve this through unbridled ambition, and they are often willing to pay almost any price to achieve their goal. Others seek to live lives of distinction vicariously through people of prominence whom they identify as heroes from stage, screen, or sports.

The thought and research that have led to *Living a Life That Counts* have revealed a great truth for me: life becomes full when you begin to give it away. A life lived in pursuit of self may lead to fame, notoriety, stardom, or even great acclaim, but never to making an existence on earth that truly counts.

In this book, I tell the stories of many people who have lived lives that have counted greatly and have been truly distinctive. The remarkable thing is that in each case this has occurred when people denied themselves and turned their lives to serving others.

I want to specifically acknowledge and thank Dr. Charles Brackett and Dr. William Williamson for training me in neurosurgery and for sharing with me their wisdom in living a meaningful life. I thank Dr. Roger Youmans, Pat Chaney, Dr. Jim Teeter, and Mae Teeter for opening their hearts to share in a personal way how God has worked in their lives.

My deep thanks go to Dr. William J. James, Dr. Dean Miller and Carol Miller, Bob Dennis, Aart and Cornelia Van Wingerden, Jerry and Dee Miller, Brother Reuben, and Dr. David Seel and Mary Seel for their example and their inspiration to me. To friends Diane Bringgold Brown and her husband, Don, as well as Rick and Dorothy Rathman, I want to express great thanks for the very personal way in which they have shared their stories.

It has been a privilege to do the Lord's work with Dr. Don Mullen and his wife, Patsy, with Carolyn and Ralph Furst, Dr. Joseph Jurisic, Rolly and Pam Laing, and Elijah and Judith Ndaruhutse. In this book they have shared experiences in which God has called them to live in service to others, and in so doing, their own lives have been blessed and made to count.

The reader will identify common threads that have been woven throughout each of the lives of these men and women of distinction. First is their humility. A second is their compassion. A third is the heeded call in each of their lives to live in service for others. Finally, each shares an awareness of the presence of God, His greatness, and the fact that through Him anything is possible.

I also want to acknowledge Dr. Billy Graham and his wife, Ruth Bell Graham, as examples of those who have demonstrated the characteristics of distinctive lives and who have been role models to me and millions of others.

Franklin Graham and his wife, Jane, have meant so much to Sylvia and me that I want to acknowledge them also. Their hearts are filled with compassion for the suffering people of this world, and they have committed their lives to carrying the gospel message and the truth of God's love to people everywhere.

My thanks to Mark Cutshall for his invaluable help—first on *Come Walk with Me* and now with *Living a Life That Counts*. As we have worked together, he has become one of my most valued friends.

These acknowledgments would not be complete without the mention of the thousands upon thousands of people who have passed my way through the years and who have impacted my life through their examples. These people are too numerous to mention by name. Some have taught me the insignificance of a life lived in attempting to please self. Others have been shining examples of how God wants us to live our lives so that we will count for others.

Finally, I want to acknowledge my wife, Sylvia, who has been faithfully at my side for thirty-seven years. Whether as a young mother tending to the needs of our own children or as a medical assistant treating long lines of sick African children in the middle of a war zone, she has always stood by my side. Standing in a crowded airport waiting to board yet another airplane to yet another place of need, or standing at the operating table in a bush hospital, Sylvia has been there at my side. My name appears as the author of this book, but it is *our* story. If through God's grace and leading our lives have counted, it has been because of what He has led the two of us to do together.

CHAPTER ONE

The Day I Began
to Live

I can still hear the words. Cold and real. Dropped into my lap without warning.

"You probably won't live beyond age fifty. You should get your living done while you can."

The doctor's voice echoed in my head. At first my mind couldn't think straight. My body knew better. I felt lightheaded. And everything in the room seemed to slow down.

"The tests show that your cholesterol is very high. People with this problem usually die early, certainly by middle age."

Questions sprang from my mouth all at once.

"Are you sure?"

"Why me?"

"Could there possibly be a mistake?"

"Isn't there something you can do about high cholesterol?"

The answers came back from the doctor as fast as my fear had raised the questions.

"Yes, we are sure. Your problem is probably congenital. No, there is no mistake. There really isn't anything you can do except quit eating eggs and fatty foods, get some daily exercise—and enjoy life while you can."

I was thirty. I was married with two small children. As I tried to take all of this in, I couldn't escape the irony that I was the doctor who did not want to accept the truth. I was nine months into my neurological surgery residency, looking forward to a career as a neurosurgeon and a future with my wife, Sylvia, and our son and daughter. And I had just learned that I probably had no more than twenty years to live.

There was no time to think about this. Outside the doctor's office, down the hall were patients I needed to visit. Patients who wanted to get well, who put their faith in a doctor who suddenly felt sad, depressed, and lost.

Afternoon dissolved into evening. Fortunately I was not on call. By nine o'clock I was home. When I opened the front door there was Sylvia. She had Michael, our sixteen-month-old, in one arm and Elizabeth, our one-month-old, in the other. After taking off my coat I sat on the couch with both children and spoke a few words I knew only they could understand. In a few minutes they fell asleep, and I returned to the moment at hand.

Over dinner I told Sylvia that I had volunteered to have some blood drawn as part of a research project at the medical center. Then I told her the results. Her disbelief matched mine. "Can't we do something about it?" she asked.

There was nothing to do. We had two small children. We were in debt. I had three more years of residency training to go, and my life would be two-thirds over before I'd be able to begin my practice.

In the span of two minutes, sitting in a doctor's office, my life had been unalterably changed by news of a chemical overload that, in 1964, medical science could barely define—much less tame. The "M.D." after my name meant nothing to this thing called "high cholesterol." This meant one thing: I would have to resign from the neurosurgery residency and get a job as a general medical doctor so I could make some money.

It was perhaps the saddest evening of my entire life. It was also the beginning of an unexpected turn of events that has since left me professionally exhilarated, emotionally exhausted, and personally fulfilled beyond what I could ever have dreamed at the time. I did not quit my neurosurgical residency and become a general practitioner. I did not die from a condition that gave me only twenty years at best to live.

That day of disbelief in the doctor's office happened in 1964, more than thirty years ago.

Today, my cholesterol level is normal, and as far as I know my health is excellent. However, this is the last you're going to hear me talk about eating fewer eggs and less bacon. Between the numbing news from the doctor and today, something incredible has come my way. It's an approach to life that's totally opposite from almost everything I learned growing up, a breakthrough that's been going on for thirty-plus years. The joy, happiness, and excitement, and the opportunities that have come as a result continue to inspire me. Now, my hope is that what I've discovered along the way can inspire you.

For the next few pages, I'm going to take off my doctor's

coat. Though I may walk you through the hospital, I am, for the purposes of this book, not a physician, but simply me. I'm a person like you. I have feelings, aspirations, and faults. I drive too fast and exercise too little. I have been known to burn a steak more than once. I still have not learned to program our VCR. Sometimes when the sun is out and I experience that rarity of a golf shot that stays in the fairway I am tempted to think I "have it together." Don't let me fool you, though. I am still trying to "get it together." If, like me, you find yourself living in both of these worlds of the "now" and "not yet," I believe there's a good chance the story you're about to read will speak to you.

Because I am one who doesn't quite yet have it all together, I can't promise you any answers. I can only leave you with a question, the question that followed me out of the doctor's office that day after learning I had only a few years to live: "What am I going to do with the rest of my life?"

That is the question I want you to sit with throughout this book. As I've become older, I've realized some people never get around to asking it. Or they wait until they are in the twilight of their years. By the time they realize they really are going to die, all but a sliver of life is behind them. I admit, except for a simple blood test, I may never have asked the question that has made all the difference. Asking and *living* this question have taken me from pursuing a *life of success* defined by status, performance, and increased emptiness to discovering a *life of significance*, which, in the last ten years, has been shaped and guided by everything opposite from what I had been taught to follow.

I'll be totally honest with you. The invitation to ask this

question is not a one-time quick fix. I've asked this question many times throughout my life. It's a little like visiting an old friend who can tell you the truth about yourself. Each time I ask myself, "What really counts in life?" I become more convinced of the answer! I've learned that asking the question doesn't depend on how much or how little I know about God. On the day I learned that cholesterol was a bad word, I believed God existed. I just didn't know He cared for me. In reality, He was there all along. Only in looking back on my life have I seen that God was present in experiences and people, and that He brought me to moments of awareness, reflection, and searching that ultimately led me to ask, "Who am I? Why am I here? Where am I going?"

As I've lived into these truths, sometimes with great joy and at other times with hesitation and trepidation, I have wanted to share them with others. But how? I couldn't just give a set of how-tos. It would be too cut and dried. Besides, life is not a recipe or a formula. You and I know there's no such thing in life as "instant reward"—just add water and stir. The other extreme of disregarding principles and simply telling my life story seemed to miss the mark as well. What good would it do to relate childhood experiences to you? How would your life be enriched by learning about the plains of Kansas—unless somehow there were kernels of life's truth waiting to be discovered? That's when the idea of this book began to sprout. The question of "What am I going to do with the rest of my life?" can't be answered by consulting an objective laundry list of to-dos. Nor can such an important matter be defined by one person's individual insights.

Between truth that can't be packaged and life that can

only be experienced I discovered a God who wanted to show me what it meant to really live. Instead of handing me formulas to follow, He accompanied me as I faced encounters with people who had forgotten more than I could ever learn. He has brought me face-to-face with experiences that were so far beyond my control I could never take credit for the blessings that followed. I wound up calling these situations "snapshots of invisible reality."

It is in these moments that my life has come into focus.

It is in these moments that I have been led to ask the all-important, unavoidable question, "What are you going to do with the rest of your life?"

It is in these moments that God has become real and present and so undeniable that to do anything less than follow His leading has been impossible. As a result of responding through my sometimes-halting, sometimes-un-questioning steps of faith, God has allowed me to see that these glimpses of reality are really not my own at all. In fact, each of the snapshots you'll read about has God's unmistakable fingerprints all over it. I believe they are really *His* glimpses, *His* way of revealing some universal truths about life, about growing up and growing old, that can speak to you and me at whatever stage of life we find ourselves. In this way, they are living analogies that reveal the God who is already at work, long before and certainly long after you and I are led, out of reflection or despera-tion, to ask the question we will explore together, "What am I going to do with the rest of my life?" I am positive that as we look at this question, you will be able to know in a fresh, perhaps surprising, way what it means to live a life that truly counts.

Deciding how you're going to live is tied to the reality

that no one really wants to admit—life is finite. Certain, unavoidable death illuminates the precious brevity of life.

Have you ever thought about your own death? Imagine being told by your doctor that you only have one month to live. At first you are shocked. But the medical evidence seems irrefutable. Your disbelief dissolves into anger and then depression. The next day, you sit down at the kitchen table with a blank piece of paper and a pen, and you begin to list all the things that have given meaning to your life. These include people, events, experiences—anything that has made life worth living.

Two weeks later, you get a call from your doctor. There was a mistake on your lab report. The true findings reveal you can expect to live about ten more years, but no more. This time, it's the real thing. For the first time, you admit to yourself that life on earth is limited and that one day you will die. It takes a while to sink in. You look at the list titled, "What has made my life meaningful to this point?" Then, to your surprise, you take another piece of paper. On the top of it you write, "What will I do with the rest of my life?"

Before you turn the page . . .

Take two pieces of paper. On the first one, list all the things that have made your life meaningful to this point. You're the only one who will ever read these words. Don't write to please someone else. Be honest. Be yourself.

After you're done, take a second piece of paper. As the above scenario suggests, imagine you have ten more years to live. Then answer the question, "What will I do with the rest of my life?" Be as specific as possible. Think in terms of how you'll invest your time, your thoughts, and your money. You may want to think of the ten years in one-year blocks.

Take some time and complete both lists now, before you read further. You'll gain more insight and appreciation from each chapter and this entire book if you do.

CHAPTER TWO

The Question We All Need to Answer Yet Seldom Ask

I must have been six. I can see my dad climbing up on top of one of the railroad refrigerator cars that rolled through the stockyards near our prairie home on a muggy summer afternoon. As a freight train stopped to take on water, he opened a trap door and crawled down inside. Then his head appeared through the opening and he lifted out a large block of ice and threw it to the ground. "Now we can freeze some ice cream after supper."

After what seemed like hours, dessert finally arrived: two large scoops of vanilla ice cream topped with chocolate sauce that ran down the sides to form a lake in the bottom of my bowl. This warm memory came to an end that night with a knock on the door that kept my dad away from the dinner table an uncomfortably long time. When he came back he was clutching a piece of paper. I had never seen his face so empty.

"It's bad news. Granddad passed away suddenly this afternoon." Granddad dead. The man who used to allow

9

me to sit on his knee as he took his pocketknife and whittled a piece of wood into a whistle. The man who had an unending list of exciting stories to tell as we sat in his big rocking chair before the warmth of the wood fire. Now, he was gone. I couldn't comprehend this. Tears ran down my face. I looked down and the mound of white ice cream with chocolate sauce on top began to blur. Ever since then I have never been able to look at a dessert like this without remembering the sadness of that day.

I was still years away from realizing my dream to be a doctor. As a child I had been mesmerized by watching a physician take my dad's blood pressure. Maybe I wanted to help people ease their suffering or prolong life. Maybe it was being so impressed with the long white coat and stethoscope. How was I to know I would one day be wearing such a coat with my name embroidered in blue script, listening to people's hearts through a stethoscope? And how was I to know that this work, this interest in caring for the human body, would find its formal beginning in a lecture room where a man wearing thick glasses, a gray seersucker suit, and a white shirt with bow tie would greet me and 107 other classmates with such wonderful news: "Good morning, I'm Dr. Paul Roof. I want you to look first to the person on your right, then to the person on your left. You can be assured that by the end of the first year, one out of three of you will have flunked out."

This was the second-most sobering moment of the day. After the introduction of several more faculty members, our class walked single file down a narrow, wooden staircase to the cellar. In this room I saw some of the first, most startling snapshots of reality that changed forever the way I looked at life.

It would be impossible to forget the smell of formaldehyde and the sight that greeted us as we walked into the cadaver morgue. There were dozens of corpses floating in the various large fluid-filled tanks. We carried one corpse at a time up those stairs and placed them on the metal tables until the dissection room was filled with twenty-seven of them. Long hours lay ahead, hours of committing to memory the intricate details of the human body. As I worked, it was with reverence and respect for the spirit of life now departed from an earthly shell. From time to time, I would pause, then return to the reality that at one time this had been the home, the vessel of a human being. This had been a small child at play. This had been a young man active in sports. Later, this remnant of a physical body was likely a loving husband and proud father. Now, all the lifetimes had met up with mine. Even this person's death had become a gift to me, a chance to inspect, ponder, and marvel at the intricate earth suit we are each given at birth.

But it wasn't until the next year in medical school that death moved from an initial state of wonderment of "what had been" to something more. It happened again in the morgue, this time in a funeral home, site of my first autopsy experience. The corpse was an attractive and obviously very pregnant young woman. She had started to feel labor pains and decided to take a bath before going to the hospital. While seated on the edge of the bathtub, she began to shave her legs with an electric razor and then reached into the bathwater to see if it was hot. Death by electrocution didn't leave much in the way of marks. And there was the double, unseen sorrow that inside this mother-to-be was a full-term baby who had come so close to experiencing the joys of living.

On a nearby table was another reminder of why I was here. He was a young man who appeared to be in a deep sleep. The mortician who had placed a pair of white tennis socks on his feet said, "He died of a broken neck after falling asleep while driving his car home for a weekend furlough. Here one minute, gone the next."

The brevity of life. And the certainty of death. Like a photo negative no one cares to look at, death was the other, unattractive, yet necessary piece to the whole picture of life. Life had escaped these people, and the questions could not escape me: What had these two young people had in mind for the rest of their lives? Why so young? What kind of person would that baby have grown up to be? What kind of mother would he or she have known? So many questions, and yet one thing remained so clear in my mind: Life was a precious gift, and because of this I gave thanks for the chance to live my life in doing all that I could to help others preserve theirs.

There was one more memorable moment in medical school in which death was my teacher, defining life and preparing me for the day I would finally admit my own mortality. En route to this lesson in my third year of medical school, I was given the opportunity to see real, live patients. How nervous could I be? After I stood in front of a very attractive young female patient with the end of my stethoscope against her chest, she said, "Excuse me, doctor. Don't you think you could hear my heart better if you placed the other ends of that thing in your ears?" I was flustered, yet confident, assuring her that "we listen, first, *without* the stethoscope in our ears, then do it again *with* the stethoscope in our ears." No scriptwriter could have written a more ridiculous explanation. No doctor could have prepared me for the script that was writing itself as I worked in the emergency room and saw life being saved and being lost.

Late one evening, the ambulance attendants brought in a middle-aged man on a stretcher and placed him in the hospital bed. "I examined him in the emergency room," the senior resident told me. "He's in end-stage renal failure. There really isn't anything we can do except keep him comfortable."

I tried my best to do so as I examined this man. He was conscious and cooperative as he gave me a medical history. In the air, however, was the strange smell of uremic poisoning. Around midnight, before going home, I came back to check on him. He was now much weaker and his breathing seemed labored.

I decided not to leave him. Instead of going home I wanted to stay at the bedside of my patient. He didn't seem to have any family except for a daughter back East. Even though I knew there was nothing I could do for him, I felt he shouldn't be alone when he died. As the night grew longer, I could see him getting progressively weaker. Yet he seldom took his eyes off mine. I knew that I was in the presence of someone who was about to die. And I knew I needed to be there when it happened.

The sun was just starting to come up when this lonely man moved his right hand slowly toward mine. I took his hand and held it as his eyelids started to become heavier by the moment. His breathing was now softer, more shallow. Then, in a seamless passage of silence, he was gone. The person who had been telling me his story the day before was no longer there. I placed the stethoscope in my ears and laid the other end against his motionless chest, then listened for a heartbeat. There was none.

I looked outside and could see the morning sun through tear-filled eyes. I was thankful to be alive. I was young, I was healthy. And I had no reason to doubt that I would live a good, long life.

Just six years later that all came to a sudden stop. On that day in 1964 when I was told I would probably die before my fiftieth birthday, I stopped assuming and started searching. Without such a point-blank wake-up call I never could have written this story of how the new awareness of death and the radical redefinition of life combined to derail the single-minded, ego-driven goal of attaining security, comfort, and wealth.

Don't let these dreams keep you from identifying with me, or from discovering that you and I are more alike than you can imagine. Remember, underneath the doctor's coat was a man who didn't know why he felt so empty when his career seemed so full. I just happened to get a taste of something so wonderful that today I'm still wanting to know more, still asking, "What will I do with the rest of my life?" The reason I keep revisiting the question is because I continue to rediscover timeless truths that have shown me how to move from leading a frantic life of business to living a life that counts.

Earlier I told you about a way God has helped me to "see" and understand these truths for myself through "snapshots of invisible reality." There are ten snapshots, ten living analogies that have helped me discover how to face the question of "What will you do with the rest of your life?" When you think about it for yourself, the implications could be a little overwhelming! And perhaps impossible to live out. It's a little like trying to take a picture of the Grand Canyon and expecting to capture its breathtaking panorama in a five-inch-wide photo. You can't. What you really need to do is *visit* the Grand Canyon. Only then can you know the reality, the awe, and the wonder. That's what God has done for me. Through a series of encounters and situations, including some that have brought deep sorrow and loss, He has walked with me. Today, I stand in awe of who He is and what He can do through simple, ordinary people who are living a boundless, freeing kind of life, much like Jesus did, reaching out to people and communities that might surprise you.

The life truths that each "snapshot" reveals are simple, yet profound. In each chapter of this book of life in walking with the Lord, you'll notice there is more than one person who plays a prominent role in the story. I did not plan it this way. Any time God has led me to a watershed moment of new understanding and new faith, He has affirmed that new reality through more than one person. One man's courageous act is illuminated by another's prayer. Even through human failure, God is there. One person's extreme virtue mushrooms into self-destruction, and we can't fully appreciate the gift of that life, now gone, until it's lived out in someone else. In each case, no person can take credit for whatever transformation takes place in your life and mine. It can only be God at work, weaving together two, three, four, or more lives to show us what's really important to us this side of heaven. No single individual can fully embody all that God has for you and me. That's why I believe when you see His invisible realities brought to life in the next few pages, you'll see a community—a neighborhood, a church, a city—being transformed by ordinary people empowered by an extraordinary God.

I have been privileged to walk beside some of these people. Their stories have given me glimpses of God's capacity to love, forgive, comfort, and give true hope that so many in our world long for. Largely because of these people, God has been developing more of Himself in me. Today, I am still being changed from the inside out. Once you meet these people I believe they will change you, because in their living and in their dying, you will see the visible proof of a God who transforms lives. Just look:

Spread out in front of me are scenes of people and events that make up a mosaic that has helped me—and I believe will help you—answer the question: "What will I do with the rest of my life?" Together they provide a peek at the discoveries that lie ahead. Individually, each photograph represents a story whose meaning is deeper now than the day it first came to light.

Have you ever wondered who has influenced your life to this point? Before I ever asked how I would live the rest of my life, there were role models. The names Grosjean, Williamson, Brackett, and James won't mean anything to you—yet. Collectively I was drawn to them like a moth to a flame. When I tell you how each imprinted a part of his character on me, I believe you'll see the people in your own life who have influenced you the most. Perhaps then, too, you will see what is fulfilling you these days. And what is not.

Have you ever reached a level of accomplishment that left you feeling exhilarated, exhausted, and somewhat empty? This is what "success" looked like to me: sleepless nights, twelve- to twenty-hour work days, five-minute lunches, and unending pressure.

There was no inspiration from watching my peers in medicine (and in all walks of life) desperately hanging on to the same merry-go-round spinning faster and faster out of control. I felt trapped: I knew the present chaos was unfulfilling, but I felt unmotivated, unprepared, and powerless to do anything about it. Without such valleys, I'm convinced we don't really start searching for what we feel is missing in our lives. Especially when you know that the time keeps ticking.

Have you ever looked up at the clock and realized, "My life is slipping away!"? As a neurosurgeon I was thrilled to be able to relieve a person's pain and prolong or even save a life. Yet I wondered, "Is there something more to life that I'm missing?" I remembered the words of my medical school dean who said, "Every successful man ought to have two careers, and the second one should begin before age fifty." It was then that I began to ask what was I going to do with the rest of my life. I might have stayed on the treadmill of success except for one word that saved me.

Have you ever dared to ask yourself, "What does *God* want me to do with the rest of my life?" This question changed everything. For me the light went on in a remote Masai village in Kenya, East Africa. I had the chance to make a difference in the world by treating patients who had never seen a doctor. What opportunity is God preparing that only you can do? There's only one way you and I can be sure.

Have you ever thought there was more than coincidence or just circumstances at work—that the rest of your life was now and He might be calling you? When I heard Franklin Graham on television describing how physicians like me were needed, a new direction for my life unfolded. The snapshot of reality that includes Franklin proved to be a crowded picture, filled with the least likely heroes who have nothing to their name but a heart of unlimited generosity. When you meet these individuals, I believe you will see the people God has put in *your* life to confirm that He has something special for you to do.

If you've ever sat up in your chair to hear a good speaker, if another person's life experience has ever caused you to say, "That's my life he's describing!" then I believe this story, this book, is for you. Not for pat solutions that don't exist, but for the freedom that comes when we risk ourselves. And for the chance to discover the question that's yours for the asking.

Look at your responses to the two questions at the conclusion of chapter 1:

"What has made my life meaningful to this point?"

"What will I do with *the rest* of my life?"

When you look at how you answered the two questions, what is the *biggest difference* in how you've lived your life to this point and how you see yourself living the next ten years? What is the *biggest similarity* in both of your responses?

Before you turn the page . . .

What are the core beliefs, attitudes, and values behind each response? In other words, what has made your life meaningful to this point in time, and what would make the next ten years worth living?

Now write out your response in no more than one paragraph (three to four sentences). As you read this book, you can expect this personal statement of who you are and what you believe to be challenged, tested, revised—and quite possibly affirmed.

CHAPTER THREE

The First Clue to a Life That Counts: Unselfishness

It can strike you in a heartbeat. Or silently creep up on you until the signs are obvious and it's too late to ignore. Something clicks. Maybe it happened to you in your early teens, or somewhere after the first year of college, or after several attempts you realized, "This is it! This is what I want to do in life. Yes, this is me."

Can you reach back into your past and find that particular moment and hold on to it? How old were you? Where were you living? Do you remember what it felt like to know you were doing exactly what you wanted? Even if it was slow in coming, I bet those feelings of confidence and determination, that sense of rightness about what you wanted to be—where you started work, whom you chose to marry—come rushing back.

Those early feelings of accomplishment are the flip side of a great lesson most people learn too late in life. I know I did. Long before I ever got around to asking the question, "What am I going to do with the rest of my life?" I began a dogged quest for self-fulfillment. I had a dream that was so virtuous I was ready to sacrifice everything. And it almost cost me. Fortunately—and here's the thing I never saw at the time—the very people who embodied this dream held the secret to my ultimate life direction. What they showed me changed the way I lived. It is such a simple yet profound truth, most people never see it, because they are too busy chasing the things they *think* will make them happy. I'd like to show you a perfect example of this: myself.

The moment you began to pursue your life's calling, you sacrificed a bit of yourself. No matter how well-motivated your goals were, you entered into something that was bigger than yourself—a company, an educational system, or realm of government. By accepting the opportunity you also accepted a culture of expectations and pressures, a set of rules that said "this is how you play the game." This is not necessarily bad. Unless the game begins to rule your life, as it did mine.

My desire to be a doctor had always been strong. As a kid, maybe I was just impressed by the stethoscope and the black medicine bag. Or the day I faced the possibility of life and death. As a sixteen-year-old, I had the chance to stand next to the operating table as my aunt underwent surgery. I can still remember that morning in the operating room as the odors of ether, antiseptic, and iodine came together as one pungent smell. That day I saw a life being saved. In Dr. Grosjean, who stood there in gown and sterile surgical gloves, his face partially covered by a surgeon's mask, I saw myself. I didn't have a clue about what I would have to give up to get there. I just wanted it. Period.

In medical school, I began to learn the rules of my game. The first year began in the classroom with eight or more hours of lectures each day, followed by eight or more hours of study each night. Two weeks into the term, we had our first quiz. I scored twenty-sixth from the bottom in a class of 120. For the next seven weeks, I spent every waking moment studying. No movies, no dates, no exercise, just hour after hour of seeking to cram every bit of information possible into my tired, aching brain. The next exam was a big one—tough—and it lasted all day. I tied for second, only a few points short from being number one.

The second year began with more classes, more labs, and more hard study. Instead of five days a week, we now went to five and a half. Instead of seven hours of sleep, I had to go to six and sometimes four. Even at mealtime, my classmates and I pored over cram cards. As the year progressed, the intensity increased, and by the end we were having two or three exams a week.

I could know more than others. I could outperform my fellow students and win the attention of a teacher. I could do and say all the right things that put me in position to climb the next rung. I could excel that little bit extra, but it still wouldn't change the rules of the game. Even though our professions may be vastly different, the same rule applies to us both: When starting out in life, you don't really know what you're in for until you dive in. Playing the game and winning was the first affirmation that what I was doing was right. But winning was not enough. I needed the natural result that comes from succeeding. I needed to be recognized. I needed to make a name for myself.

At the time I didn't realize what was shortsighted about this approach. I couldn't see anything wrong because, for an intense, goal-oriented person like me, the ego is invisible. Have you seen your ego at work lately? You can be sure it's putting in overtime when

- you find a special pleasure impressing others with who you are and what you know;

- your goal is not to do your best but to beat everyone else; and

- once you have proved yourself this way, it's still not enough.

Thanks to my ego, I began to master all of these without even trying.

Being successful at the game took time and an all-out desire to win. I was driven to learn more, to score higher. There was no greater challenge than to learn what everyone else knew and then a little extra. This was the intoxicating game of one-upmanship. On early morning rounds in the hospital, the professor discussed patients' charts with our group of medical students. At just the right moment, I would drop a pearl of wisdom to impress the others, then feel the adrenaline rush and the accompanying smirk of superiority spread across my face. Another student would then counter with his pearl of wisdom, and the intellectual race continued. When Dr. Frank Albritten, the professor and chairman of the Department of Surgery, offered me a residency to begin after graduation from medical school and a year of internship, I knew I was winning the game. It was all about professional pride, not the promise of making money. It was reaching for the goal the faculty always stressed: to be excellent in medicine as a knowledgeable, caring physician. After graduating from medical school, I was ready to keep winning.

This time the game was internship, an additional year of training that would prepare me to begin a five-year residency program of specialization. The rule was to apply to five or ten of the top hospitals in the country and let a computer-matching program do the rest. But I applied to only one, the University of California in San Francisco (UCSF). "Are you out of your mind? That's a very difficult place to get into," my professors and fellow students told me. What a thrill it was to receive the letter of acceptance. I had stared the competition in the face and had come out on top again.

During those last months of medical school, I had made a slight adjustment in my priorities, feeling confident enough to de-emphasize the focus on the "big G"—grades—and to find time for the other "big G"—girls. I felt more blessed than ever when God brought a beautiful young lady named Sylvia into my life. Born and educated in London, she had come to America to fly for TWA. On the day before medical school graduation, she became my wife.

What rewards do you get from "playing the game"? A spouse? A professional degree? A big-time promotion? An ulcer? A drinking problem? An empty marriage? A costly divorce? You probably know someone who played the game of trying to get ahead—and lost. My experience is that people will keep striving, keep reaching, unless something comes along that stops them in their tracks. By the time I was twenty-five years old that moment had not yet come. I was too busy with my initial conquest: M.D.

A number of years ago, I was invited to a dinner to hear the president of Cal Tech speak. In the world of premier scientific education and research, it's no secret that the name Cal Tech rhymes with genius. After the address, he fielded questions from the audience. One man asked, "I wondered, when you spoke to the student body, what was it like to know you were speaking to a group of men and women who had scored perfect 1600s on their SAT tests?" He smiled and replied, "To be honest, there was no pressure at all. You see, as a student, I had a perfect 1600 myself."

Without knowing it, of course, he had described what I had found in my fellow interns at UCSF. To call them superachievers was an understatement. These people were brilliant. I would try to seize the opportunity to drop a pearl of wisdom and realize they were already holding the pearl. Now, winning meant just being able to keep up with sharp individuals who would do anything to get ahead and pass you by. One morning, for instance, during my first month, the flu suddenly caught up with me. I was the intern who was assigned to work with Dr. Leon Goldman, the chairman of the Department of Surgery. The first operation, of many, was scheduled to begin at 8:00 A.M. I remember announcing that I felt ill that morning. Within minutes, three or four of my fellow interns appeared to volunteer to take my place at the operating table. As I did, they wanted to make a name for themselves. They wanted to be noticed by "the Chief."

A few weeks later, as I was making patient rounds with Dr. Goldman, he offered me some advice. "Get up at 4:30 each morning and go to the hospital laboratory to get all of the latest test results on each patient. When the other doctors arrive at 5:30, you will already be one step ahead of them, prepared to lead the race all day, rather than follow with the others."

Earning the title of M.D. and being an intern meant this kind of sacrifice and discipline. Had Dr. Goldman suggested I wake up at 4:00 or even 3:30 in the morning, I probably would have gone right ahead and set my alarm clock. I was willing to do anything to earn the title. I never asked the question, "How much is too much?" Have you asked yourself this question? Are you willing to set limits? For the most part I was not. I don't have a neatly packaged pearl of wisdom for how to balance your life. What helped me see beyond my own driven nature was a person.

When I began my residency in general surgery, the salary was only two hundred dollars a month, but I would have worked for nothing just for the thrill and personal rewards of my profession. Now I had a medical license and I was a "real doctor." I assisted in surgery almost nonstop for a year. The responsibilities were greater than I had ever dreamed. The work was hard and the hours incredibly long. Logically speaking, the physical and emotional pressures should have consumed me. Instead they fueled my desire to become a neurosurgeon. It meant shifting to a new residency program—a move inspired by a professor I had come to like, respect, and admire more than I can describe. His name was Charles E. Brackett, Jr., M.D. The gift of genius, coupled with his vision for new research and developments in the young field of neurosurgery, greatly inspired me. When he lectured to medical students or residents, it was with enthusiasm and brilliance, yet with clarity that made learning fun.

Dr. Brackett was the professor, the visionary, the mentor, and the friend who opened the door to the discoveries that spoke to my curiosity as if to say, "Come closer, there's so much more for you to learn." Several things were at work inside me. Neurosurgery was a relatively new and undeveloped specialty. There seemed to be no end to the number of patients who needed surgical treatment for brain and spinal cord injuries. Then there were the patients who harbored brain tumors or suffered from hydrocephalus, strokes, pain, or other conditions for which there seemed to be so few answers.

It was easy to be impressed by how much certain doctors knew about the brain. They had earned the title of "neurosurgeon." But what impressed me more was the person who used his title to save a life. Several months into my general surgery residency year, I was paged to come to the office of Dr. Williamson, Chief of Neurosurgery. His secretary, Rowena, was cordial yet firm when I arrived in the doorway. "Dr. Cheatham, we don't have your application for neurosurgical residency. If you're going to apply for our program, we need it soon."

After years of working sixteen-hour days, I didn't look forward to ten- and twelve-hour operations and four more years of residency training. And there was the "D" word always looming in discussions about the specialty of neurosurgery. The frequency of death and the sense of depression created by so many patients in coma were well known among practicing neurosurgeons. The lack of positive conversation was so real, they would joke to each other, "Hey, I'm going to go make patient rounds. How about coming with me so that I will have someone to talk to."

In an attempt to finally make up my mind and apply, I left Dr. Williamson's office and headed to the operating room where I knew he would be at work. Activity was buzzing about the special operation about to take place that day. The patient was a woman who had suffered a ruptured aneurysm deep under the brain in the center of her head. This was, literally, a life-and-death situation. The chance of survival for ruptured aneurysms at that time was no better than 50 percent. The small ballooning out of the artery (which constitutes an aneurysm) is like a thin bubble waiting to pop. When the constant pulsating pounding of the blood against the artery finally causes it to burst, the resultant hemorrhage is often fatal. If death is not immediate, a second or third hemorrhage will likely be the crippling blow.

In 1961, before the use of surgical microscopes in neurosurgery, the operation was so complicated that it demanded the talents of two surgical teams. The plan was set: cardiac surgeon Dr. Frederick Kittle and his team would cool the patient's body to slow the metabolism and the heart function to the point of near cardiac arrest. Then, Dr. Williamson would open the head and quickly place a small metal clip on the aneurysm under the brain to keep it from bleeding.

After giving the woman a general anesthetic, they lowered her into a horse trough filled with ice water and carefully monitored her body functions as her temperature began to fall. At about 86 degrees Fahrenheit, the patient was moved back onto the operating table, and her temperature was dropped even lower to a cold 33 degrees Celsius, until her heart was nearly ready to stop beating. Dr. Williamson and his resident, Dr. Bill Smith, quickly cut open the scalp and laid it down over the face like a curtain. Then they removed a large part of the front of the skull, gently lifted up the front of the cerebral hemispheres, and temporarily clipped the major arteries to the front of the brain.

The entire surgical team of perhaps fifteen surgeons, anesthesiologists, nurses, and technicians was tense as the surgeons worked against the clock. As I stood watching neurosurgical history being made, my own heart was pounding fast. With precision, Dr. Williamson made the skillful, unforgiving movement, placing the silver clip across the base of the aneurysm. "Mission accomplished," he said as he momentarily stepped back from the operating table and took a long, deep breath.

If this was going to be the neurosurgery of the future, I had to be a part of it. After surgery I couldn't walk fast enough down the hall to take my signed application for neurosurgical residency to Dr. Williamson's office. I was eager to work with him and Dr. Brackett, the two people who, more than anyone else, would impact my career.

Learning the science of medicine could come from textbooks, but understanding how to live one's life as a doctor of medicine had to be learned from other physicians. If Dr. Brackett had stirred my curiosity for learning, Dr. William P. Williamson showed me an approach to life I had never considered. Like me, if you've ever tired of playing the game or earning a title, it will jump out at you. The irony is that this man, who was so brilliant when it came to understanding the workings of the human brain, taught me so much about the depth and caring of the human heart. To me, he defined "mentor" before the word ever came into vogue. And in keeping with his humility, he was unaware of what he imparted to me.

It was a calm, breezy April evening. My work at the University of Kansas Medical Center had kept me running all day, and would likely continue through the night. At around 9:00 P.M., Sylvia arrived to join me for dinner in the hospital lobby. She had prepared some sandwiches and packed them in a little overnight bag. I was on call and couldn't leave the hospital, so my dinner break was at least a chance to be together. Since this was as close as Sylvia had come to experiencing my world as a physician, I had an idea.

"Would you like to go upstairs to the operating room and see Dr. Williamson do a brain operation?" I asked.

She stopped midway in taking a bite from her sandwich. "Me, watch a brain operation?! Are you kidding?"

"I know the best seat in the house," I said. "There's a viewing gallery with a glassed-in wall up above the neuro-surgery operating room. We can watch together." And we did. What I was about to see was a picture, a snapshot of the timeless truth that serving other people is at the heart of living a life that counts.

The patient was a dark-haired, but graying, woman in her forties with a depressed skull fracture. The collision force of a near-fatal car accident had caused her to hit her right forehead against the dashboard. The blow had frac-tured her skull, driving some of the pieces of bone into the brain. Otherwise, she was conscious and alert. Dr. Williamson would go inside her brain and extract the bone fragments—under local anesthesia with the patient awake!

I scooted up to the edge of my chair. I felt I was watching my future as a neurosurgeon unfold. Here was the surgeon, soon to be my mentor, the professor who had first inspired me during medical school and who, along with Dr. Brackett, would lead me to my goal of becoming "a brain surgeon."

After shaving the woman's head, and scrubbing the bald scalp with soap and water, Dr. Williamson applied iodine. Then he covered all but the front part of her scalp with sterile sheets. As he picked up the needle that held the local anesthetic, I could hear his Arkansas accent.

"Now, ma'am," he said, "I'm going to put a little bit of medicine into the skin. It's going to feel like a little bee sting, but it really won't hurt much. It's just like being in the dentist's chair. Now, don't you be nervous or bothered. Everything will be just fine."

Taking the knife, he made a curved incision from just in front of the right ear, up to the middle of the scalp and then down to the forehead. Blood began to run down the scalp, down the drapes, then onto the floor. After dissecting the scalp away from the skull, he retracted it forward over the patient's right eye. We could begin to see the skull, broken in pieces and pushed into the head like a dent in a Ping-Pong ball.

"Now, ma'am, you're going to feel a little pressure, but it won't hurt. I'm going to drill several holes in your skull. If you have any pain, you just tell me 'cause I don't want to hurt you."

I didn't know which was more remarkable: the careful precision of the surgeon's hands or the folksy, affirming way he eased his anxious patient. At the heart of this brilliant physician was a human being who knew how to relate to others.

I turned and looked at Sylvia's face. Her eyes were fixed on the operation. I knew she was witnessing something she never, in her wildest dreams, would have imagined seeing.

Dr. Williamson said, "Now, there'll be a little noise while I drill. You'll hear a little grinding. But don't you move."

A small, anxious whimper leaked out of the woman's mouth. "Aren't I going to feel it? Won't it hurt?" she asked.

"No, ma'am. You can trust me. If there's any time you feel uncomfortable, you just let us know. We don't want you to be at all uncomfortable. Hold still now—don't you move."

And so the conversation went. The doctor talking, listening, then comforting his patient—in the middle of her own brain surgery! It was both bizarre and a compassionate exchange of concern and understanding between two people. In a way, Dr. Williamson, who had been my professor in medical school, was the teacher once again. This time his textbook illustration just happened to be a real person.

For the next forty-five minutes, Dr. Williamson worked to remove the dark, clotted blood and the fragments of bone from his patient's brain. Then he repaired the torn lining of the brain and wired the pieces of fractured skull back in place where they could heal and once again offer protection. After he sewed the scalp back together with an interlocking stitch, the woman's head looked a little bit like a baseball. Once the wound had a chance to heal, and the hair grew back, no one would ever guess that she had suffered a life-threatening head injury.

"Ma'am, we are finished operating, and you are doing just fine," said Dr. Williamson as he removed the sterile drapes and wrapped the head in bulky gauze dressing. "Everything went very well. Except for a little headache, I think you're going to be up and about tomorrow without any problem." Then, almost as if apologizing for a major inconvenience, he saw the shaved area on the woman's scalp. "I'm sorry, ma'am, but we had to shave your hair off." He removed his surgical mask and smiled at the lady. "Maybe when your hair grows back in, it will be blond and curly." The smile that spread across the woman's face must have been more than enough to pay Dr. Williamson for what he had done for her.

In the operating room that evening, I saw the first clues to what made Dr. Williamson tick. Something made him different, but what? The doctors I looked up to during my training exploited their talent to the max. They were intellectual giants who excelled either in teaching, actual practice, or research, or at times, all three. Some were so aware, so sure of their own abilities, they made sure you knew it. Had they been my only examples, I would have thought medicine was a factual discipline, a technical challenge of fixing people's problems with the right answers. But Dr. Williamson showed me otherwise.

He helped me see that doctors didn't just work from facts; they touched people where they lived. This was never clearer than the time Dr. Williamson was touched himself. He took a two-month vacation from the medical center and spent the time as a volunteer on board the hospital ship *Hope*. For someone who had grown up in rural

Arkansas, who had enjoyed a comfortable life free from sickness, those months in Peru proved shocking. Every morning, long lines of barefoot villagers suffering from a wide assortment of diseases stood in line waiting to board the ship. Many wouldn't live to see their fiftieth birthday. All were in desperate need of medical help. But when Dr. Williamson recounted the experience to me, he wasn't thinking medicine.

"Mel, those people don't need a brain surgeon. They need soap and clean water. They need to learn about basic sanitation. They need help in learning to grow crops so that they will have adequate food to eat." In Peru, as he saw how poverty bleeds the human spirit, Dr. Williamson took off his white starched shirt and took on a new outlook about life. It seemed as if his heart had been massaged by the husbandless women and the crying children whom the world of modern medicine would probably never touch. I could only listen to his stories and think that something had gotten inside the man. I knew it had to do with his beliefs as a Christian. He talked about his duty, his responsibility as a person who believed in God. At the time I nodded politely. Back then I didn't see it. I didn't see the reasons for giving that Dr. Williamson obviously felt. But that day came.

Near the end of the four years I spent working with Dr. Williamson, his passion for the needs and the hurts of others nearly changed my life. One day a little boy was brought in experiencing severe headaches, vomiting, and fever. He rapidly lapsed into a deep coma. Within twelve hours he died of encephalitis. Dr. Williamson took me with him to attend the little boy's funeral. On that blustery winter day, it seemed even colder inside the church than outside. After the service, still freezing, I couldn't wait for Dr. Williamson to turn on the small heater inside his Volkswagen Beetle. Both of us hopped inside and shut the doors. Then, instead of starting the engine, he began to unload his feelings from the funeral. He reminisced about the little boy who had been so happy and so active until illness suddenly struck. He talked about the fragility of life. Meanwhile my teeth were chattering, but I said nothing. With deep conviction, he talked about the need to care for hurting people as I felt the imitation-leather seats begin to crack under my numb legs. He would almost put the key in the ignition, and then another thought would come to him. This went on until I was bouncing my feet up and down on the floor mat.

"You know, Mel, where that little boy is right now, there is no suffering or sorrow. It's not there." I thought to myself, *Dr. Williamson, if you keep talking much longer, I'm going to freeze to death, and end up there with the little boy, where there's no suffering or sorrow.*

It may have been the most vivid memory of our friendship, though not the most poignant. That took place after what seemed like a lifetime of study at the University of Kansas Medical Center. It was my last day of training. Before leaving for California, where I would begin my private practice, I went to Dr. Williamson's office to thank him and to say good-bye. We stood there looking at each other shaking hands. Each time I started to let go, he only tightened the grip of his hand on mine.

"Mel, I can't tell you how much I've enjoyed you as my resident. I have great empathy with you." Though I didn't know what he meant, we stood there for a long moment looking at each other. Then he simply smiled and said,

"Good luck to you, and God bless you." I couldn't have known that it was the last time I would see him alive.

Three months later, Sylvia, the kids, my parents, and I unlocked the door and walked into our home in Ventura, California. We had just enjoyed a weekend vacation in San Diego.

Then the telephone rang.

It was the answering service telling me that Dr. Charles Clough, my friend from neurosurgery residency days in Kansas City, had called. I dialed his number right away. The moment I heard his voice I knew something was wrong.

"Mel, I've got some bad news. Really, some very bad news. Dr. Williamson died several hours ago."

And that was how the relationship with a gifted mentor came to an end. That night I cried uncontrollably. It was like losing a teacher, a father, and a friend all in one unexpected blow. Two days later at the funeral, the sun was shining. And inside the church it was warm. A memory was burning. I could see Dr. Williamson. We would be examining a case, and my analysis would be wrong. I had miscalculated and tried dropping a pearl of wisdom instead of listening and learning. Suddenly, I could see his face and hear his words. "Mel, that's your lesson in humility for today." That was the real genius of the man. Always teaching, always reminding me that no matter how smart I thought I was, there was always someone a little bit smarter. His intention wasn't to put me down. His goal was to show me a quiet little truth that's so easy to miss: When you're humble is when you can best serve.

Serving others. Putting others above self, not out of courtesy, but from conviction. This is what motivated Dr.

Williamson to practice medicine, to help the poor, and to help a young aspiring physician named Mel Cheatham. Service that's fed by humility is the forgotten truth that reinvigorates life. Instead of taking from others it gives. Instead of looking for a way out it seeks a way under, over, or around to help another person in need.

Before we can ask the question, "What will I do with the rest of my life?" we must ask ourselves, "What's driving my life right now?" Want to know the answer? Just ask yourself these three questions:

- What things do I think about most often?
- How do I spend my free time?
- How do I spend my money?

What things are at the top of your list? Like most people, I didn't like what I saw at the top of my list. I didn't admit my unhappiness to myself because I didn't know what was missing.

Only when I met a person who committed his life to serving others did I realize there must be more to life than trying to please myself.

Most of us don't disagree that service is a higher virtue than self-reward. Instead, we get stuck on how to change if, in fact, we even dare. We know what will happen if we ever give up control of our careers, our spouses, our children, our future. We'll lose ourselves! Believe me, I've seen it happen. Not once, but continually over a period of years. Not with one person, but two.

Dr. William Williamson "gave away" his own medical career to help the poor who could never possibly repay him. Dr. Charles Brackett gave away his enthusiasm and vision: "Mel, you can accomplish anything you want in life. It's all there just waiting for you." And for thirty-five years since, Dr. Brackett has continued to be a friend and a model for serving others.

When the University of Kansas School of Medicine needed a new hospital, it was Dr. Charles Brackett whom they named dean and provost. His leadership in neurosurgery, both in America and abroad, has been invaluable to the growth of this highly skilled specialty. Thirty-five years after he first became my friend and inspiration, I was privileged to be with him as he was awarded the Distinguished Service Award by his peers, neurosurgeons from around the world who had been blessed by his example of living a life that counts.

There is probably someone in your life who has given himself or herself away to you. What is it he or she has done that you'll never forget? What bit of his or her character, values, and life are you glad to call your own? Think about that person's life. And be grateful. You have what so many people today long for: an example, a mentor, a living reminder of the fact that you can still find a piece of heaven on earth. This is made even more special when you realize that the currency of this world is money; the currency of heaven is relationships.

Many people measure the significance of their lives by what they have accomplished. For others, life's true value is found in the people they have come to know, trust, love, and serve.

The fact is that we value life both because of what we do and because of whom we share our life with. Often what gets lost is the other fact—that what you're able to do is *because* someone invested himself or herself in you.

Before you turn the page . . .

Imagine you had to write the definition for one word in an upcoming new dictionary. The word is *unselfish*. Instead of relying on what past dictionaries have said, write your definition of *unselfish* based on a person in your life who showed you the meaning of the word. Think of a memorable experience or action from this person's life that you can express so that anyone who reads your definition will say, "Now, *that's* what it means to give yourself to someone else." If you have trouble coming up with such a person, think of an unforgettable character from a movie, book, or story. By giving a few minutes of your own time to this unselfish person and his or her life example, you'll appreciate the meaning of chapter 4.

CHAPTER FOUR

The Disease That May Be Robbing You of Your Future Right Now

She was only nineteen years old when I met her, lying on the stretcher as the emergency medical team lifted her from the back of the ambulance. I can still see her dark brown hair, the deep brown eyes, the right pupil widely dilated, staring but not really seeing. Around her neck was a small gold chain. And blood was running from her right ear. Her name was Sandra, and she had no idea she was facing the final minutes of her life.

As they wheeled her inside the emergency room, she was in a race she couldn't win. Moments before she had been laughing on the back of a motorcycle. She must have felt the wind in her hair, the sun on her face—she probably hadn't even seen it coming. The car that didn't stop, the bike that did. Before she could turn her head, it was too late.

Now, a deep coma had changed the rules of life. I doubted she would ever open her eyes again. But I was the doctor, and I had to try. We inserted a tube down her

39

trachea so she could breathe, placed her on a respirator, then rushed her to the operating room. I ran alongside the gurney, cutting hair away from her head in order to save precious seconds we would need if we were to save her life.

Standing beside the operating table, looking down on this young woman I would never know, I saw how fragile, how vulnerable life really is. Through the next two hours of surgery I saw that the brain damage was beyond repair. This time, as on so many other unwelcome occasions, death left its silent signature in a straight, green line on a heart monitor. As I sat on a stool long enough to write what was necessary on the chart, I looked at Sandra's face and thought of the rest of her life she would now never know. The career that would never be. Perhaps children who now would never be born.

The enemy that had taken it all away had been bigger than the physician, bigger than medicine, bigger than life. In that moment of reflection, death began to teach me about life once again. I thought of another enemy that's also stealing life from many other young people Sandra's age, a "disease" so subtle you could have been carrying it for years and not even know it.

It strikes people at any time in life. It has nothing to do with what you eat and everything to do with what you feed your mind and your heart. The biggest symptoms are indifference and neglect. If you have never asked yourself the question, "What am I going to do with the rest of my life?" there's a better than 90 percent chance you're vulnerable to this other enemy. Even if you have seriously considered your future, there's still a better than fifty-fifty chance of being struck. People approaching midlife and beyond have more to worry about than those under thirty.

If you haven't reached the big three-oh, you are in the best position to recognize the symptoms. Most people don't see them. You may not either, unless you know where to look.

If I came right out and told you the name of this largely unrecognized, widespread "disease," you might ignore the evidence and say, "That doesn't apply to me. I'm doing just fine, thank you." But if I give you the chance to discover the "disease" yourself, I have no doubt you will do some things differently with your life before you finish this book. In fact the best way to know this enemy, and thereby avoid it, is to look at its major cause, that of *not* asking yourself, "What am I going to do with the rest of my life?"

Close your eyes and become twenty-five years old for a moment. How far back (or forward!) did you have to go? Look at the person you were, or hope to become.

- What are you wearing?
- Where are you living?
- What does your day look like? Your job? Your home? Your weekend?
- What one thing are you focused on more than anything else?

Hold on to this picture, because what you see and feel in this image is what your life is really all about. There's a good chance this freeze-frame of your young adult years was (or is) filled with transition and transformation. That's because the early and mid-twenties are a cyclone of change. How many anxious departures and arrivals can you remember? Leaving home for college. Leaving college for the first job. Moving into the new apartment. Friends getting married. And life getting more complicated. The securities of childhood—parents, neighborhood, and friends—slip away as we feel our way into adulthood. No one is quite sure when it happens, but many are sure the transformation starts about the time you first see your name on a monthly phone bill. Somewhere along the way, you decide what it is you're going to do with your life, or you let outside forces such as a boss, obligation, or guilt dictate where you work, what you buy, and with whom you spend time. Two things are certain: The first is that at no other time in life do you have such freedom to decide. The second is that as you leave decisions in the hands of others, they, and not you, will answer the question of "What will you do with the rest of your life?" *for* you.

Unfortunately, most people in their early adulthood aren't even aware the question exists. Their circuits are too swamped and their energy too drained from responding to two basic human instincts that drive all of life. The first is satisfying the basic needs for survival in a hostile world. To modern-day creatures like you and me, it's the satisfaction that comes from finding a new apartment to rent or landing the first bite of dinner after you've gone all day without food.

The second fundamental instinct is to satisfy the urge for power and money. As a young doctor eager to get established, I struggled trying to choose between the two. In the process of deciding, I met a person who showed me a motivation for living that made me wonder why I was working for either one. Without trying to, he showed me that I was already living with the early stages of the "disease," and it was already eating away at my life.

As the time drew close for me to complete my neurosurgical residency, Dr. Brackett offered me an opportunity to stay on the faculty as an instructor in neurosurgery. My close friend from school days, Dr. John Chapman, was then associate dean of the medical school, and he offered to pave the way for me to become an assistant dean. The thought of becoming a full professor someday—and being the dean of a medical school, while the pay was modest, translated into the highest level of academic achievement. But the intoxicating lure of money and the security it would buy was equally strong. At thirty-four, I had built up large debts and put off the personal gratification of material comforts too long. Power and money. I couldn't satisfy my urge for both. After a great deal of soul-searching, I chose to go into private practice in California where I could make much more money.

I never questioned my desire to earn a generous income. I had responsibilities—debts to pay off and a family to raise. Without knowing it, I became a slave to the anxious voice inside that said, "There's still a little bit more to do, so get busy." It was another, unexpected anxiety, however, that really shook me up.

I felt it whenever I thought of my two mentors, Drs. Brackett and Williamson. By the time I was in my final year of training, both men had made a deep imprint upon me in ways I didn't fully understand. Both showed me that I could earn a living as a physician. But what really drew me to them was their deep desire to help others, their unmistakable integrity, and an approach to life that seemed so right and good. For them, medicine was far more than a way to make a living. It was an ongoing expression of how life was meant to be lived—serving others rather than serving self. For them, helping people was just as important as, maybe more important than, building a successful medical practice.

It was safe to admire my mentors. I could look up to them without having to sacrifice my goals, my dreams, or my desires to be like them. I could have joined Dr. Williamson on the hospital ship *Hope* to help the poor in South America, but not if it meant postponing my career. Besides, no one my age, no peer or acquaintance I knew, was willing to sacrifice his or her own earning potential in order to do charitable work. No one, that is, until I met Roger Youmans.

He was a fellow surgical resident, a friend, and a nagging dilemma. Even if I had wanted to ignore Roger Youmans, I couldn't. His personality was irresistible. And the things he and his wife, Mary, were involved in only puzzled me. Why, for instance, did they feel such a deep compassion for the sick and the suffering? What were they doing wanting to be Christian medical missionaries in Africa? I'd look at him and think to myself, *How can you give up the good life here at home and go to the jungle and live in some hut?* I didn't get it. Why would someone my age choose to give up financial security, comfort, and professional gain to work for nothing? Of course I didn't want Roger to know what I was really thinking: *Oh, I know what you're doing is right, but it's not for me. Not now.*

Yes, but . . .

In the space of two tiny words, I exposed myself to a quiet, troubling disease. What I didn't realize then was that life-changing opportunities live and die in the time it takes to say "Yes, but . . ." You may put yourself at risk and not even know it. Sometime in the last six months a Roger Youmans has crossed your path. It may have been a classmate, a pastor, a longtime relative, or a close friend.

In them you saw something you admired. For a moment you allowed yourself to dream. The opportunity, the challenge, the goal, everything inside you said "Yes!" Then, once the rush of excitement boiled over, your dream cooled to doubt and you thought, "Yes, but . . ." In that moment of seeing what you might have to give up, you exposed yourself to the hidden "disease" I myself carried as a young, aspiring physician. By saying, "Not now, not yet, not me, Lord," you became weakened by the "disease" called "I can't."

"I can't" usually strikes the brain and spreads throughout the person's entire attitude. I know, because I've lived with it for over sixty years. Yet it doesn't take a physician to spot the symptoms you may have already noticed in yourself:

"I can't take this job. It just feels too risky, too uncomfortable, too hard."

"I can't say yes to that leadership opportunity at church. I don't really have the time."

"It's too overwhelming. I'd be all alone."

"It's not worth the risk."

"Sorry, I can't."

People are able to live with the disease "I can't" for years. What many don't realize, what *I* didn't realize most of the time, is that very slowly, very unsuspectingly, the words "I can't" can rob you of pivotal opportunities in life that may come around only once. Believe me, I'm all for learning how to say no. People who don't learn how to say no spend their lives frantically reacting to the unending demands of others. "I can't" is something totally different. When you say "I can't," you're saying, "Sorry, I'm unavailable" to the chance to grow. When you say "I can't," you let go of an opportunity—an opportunity to leave the comfort and security of base camp and make the climb that rewards the risk with a view most never see. That climb, that risk in front of you, is the unresolved decision you went to sleep with last night. It's the phone call you've been putting off, the choice to which one half of you says, "This is right," and the other half asks, "What am I doing?"

"But Mel," you say, "the last thing I'm going to do is put my future and my family's security at risk. I agree that God wants us to be faithful, but I don't think He wants us to be continually stressed out by thinking I could always be doing something more with my life."

For twenty years after I started my own practice I said, "I can't" for a thousand different reasons. For twenty years I allowed the need for financial security, family security, and professional stability to run my life. By the time I was fifty I had all the security, all the money, all the recognition I thought would make me happy. But I wasn't happy. Something was missing, something I had seen in my mentors in medical school but didn't yet know for myself. That "something" was the wonderfully freeing desire to serve other people without gain for myself. This is the lesson I almost discovered too late: *Unless you learn that serving others is just as essential as your own security, unless you develop the habit of giving your time, talents, and treasure to someone else, you may never know what God had in store for you in this life.*

Today, some of the most contented, relaxed, and fulfilled people I know are those who learned this truth *while their best years were still before them*. What makes these people different from the ones who become frustrated and ultimately defeated by saying "I can't"? The answer may surprise and encourage you, especially when you discover the incredible risk and sacrifice these people have overcome.

I told you how much I had admired Roger Youmans for helping the poor and sick in Africa when he could have been earning a comfortable living in this country. For six years in Zaire, another two in Ghana, and five months in Swaziland, he and his wife, Winky, served the poor, the sick, and the disadvantaged. Even their small children had joined in the work of ministering to the needs of others. The most inspiring moment of his time in Africa came unexpectedly. The year was 1961. Roger left his family in America for six months of missionary service in the Belgian Congo. Here he was the only doctor for a nation being pulled apart by civil war.

Weeks before he arrived, Simba rebels had slashed their way through his village killing any natives they believed had come in contact with Western missionaries. In the midst of this violence, Roger chose to serve the innocent victims of war. He had taken a group of men and women fresh out of college into this uncharted mission territory where medical treatment was as rare as a cease-fire. In the face of gunfire, the talk among the villagers was not of war but of building a hospital and spiritual revival. Crews arrived before dawn to clear trees, dig foundations, and pour concrete. By early afternoon the temperature climbed to well over 100 degrees and the humidity only made it worse. Roger was not immune from working these hours, which started with giving the morning devotions at five o'clock each day.

I remember seeing the faces of 150 men and women who had walked through the early morning darkness with kerosene lanterns to build a hospital and clear land for a revival meeting. They knew at any time they could be shot at and killed. I stood before these people and wondered what I could possibly say to parents who had seen their children die and who had still come back to literally clear a place for God's work. I felt so inadequate. Here I had come to Africa as a messenger of the gospel. And when my eyes met theirs on that dark, muggy morning, I wondered if my words really mattered.

At that moment, feeling so empty inside, I came back to the one thing I knew for sure: all of us in that room had been rescued from our own sinful selves by Jesus Christ. Whatever happened to any of us that day in the steamy, fear-filled Congo, we could know we were loved forever by God. In the dim-lit morning we could still see the cross.

Sometimes a feeling of inadequacy can make us feel defeated and concerned over all the things we think we lack. We allow our perceived lack of ability to minimize our own self-worth and our true worth to God. Instead of succumbing to this false conclusion, Roger Youmans discovered something different. Knowing and sharing God's love don't depend on what we feel. Even when we feel we're in over our head, God is totally adequate to use faithful and imperfect people to communicate His total, unconditional love found in Jesus Christ.

Roger realized that only through his emptiness could God fill him with the humility necessary for Christian service. In the years that followed, he and Winky spent many months caring for the diseased and suffering in Central Africa. The reason they were able to risk their health, safety, and future is the same reason you can risk saying yes to whatever opportunity God has put before you: There's a world out there filled with people who need what you have to give them. I know a schoolteacher who discovered this truth when she discovered her own inadequacy.

Pat Chaney teaches fifth grade at Saticoy School in Ventura, California. Look into the eyes of her students and you will learn why she has stayed in the classroom for the past twenty-two years: Rakesh from India can speak fluent Punjabi, but barely speaks English. Manuel was born with fetal alcohol syndrome. Though he is thirteen years old, his reading level is that of a third grader. Jodie, an orphan from Korea, has cerebral palsy. Her mammoth language, cultural, and learning challenges have just begun. The list goes on. Thirty-three children with unique needs, thirty-three reasons their teacher experiences regular waves of frustration and feeling overwhelmed. Pat's tears began over twenty years ago when her niece, Janell, was just one year old and doctors discovered a mild form of cerebral palsy. She was handicapped for life. She would not grow up like most little girls. Says Pat:

> For months I cried off and on, asking "Why, God? Why Janell?" Then, on the first day of school one year, the principal at Penfield School for multihandicapped children, a school right across the street from Saticoy, brought his daughter into my class. That next week my students began volunteering as teacher's aides at Penfield. Though they are just ten years old, they know their assignments: Jeremy helps feed a quadriplegic girl who cannot raise a spoon to her mouth; Martin helps a young boy his own age learn to add and subtract; Kelly makes

sure the chalkboard is clean and that every child has a book for that morning's reading lesson.

I think of my niece, Janell. In all those years of asking "Why, God?" I didn't know that God was preparing me for something I couldn't chalk up to coincidence.

Back in her own classroom, Pat learned, again, the lessons of patience and giving that her niece's condition had been teaching her for years. One day a girl named Lydia walked into Pat's classroom. Her family had fled Los Angeles after receiving threats from gang members. "This was a girl whose study skills were almost nil," recalls Pat. "She could barely write her own name. All the years with Janell had helped me look beyond Lydia's outward condition to the real person—the willing little girl who wanted to learn. I told Lydia, 'I don't care where you start, if you stick with me you're going to succeed.' I pushed her to do her best. Sometimes she got angry, but I told her to never stop trying. And she never did."

On the last day of the school year, all the students in Pat Chaney's fifth-grade class lined up at the door to leave for the final time. Pat stood at the door and told each child what he or she had meant to her. With her words and hugs she told each child, "You're important. You matter to God, and you matter to me." She waved good-bye to one child, turned back to the line, and there was Lydia. She stood in front of her teacher, looked at her for a brief moment then put her arms around the woman who had helped her learn to read and study for the first time. Though Pat couldn't see Lydia's face, she could hear the cracked voice. "Miss Chaney, I love you so much. I'm going to make you proud of me."

"I'm *already* proud of you," said Pat. Lydia began to cry. Pat Chaney held on to her student, afraid to let go because, inside, she began to cry. She thought of what she had told Lydia and the rest of her students on the first day of class: "You know, we're all handicapped. I wear glasses for my handicap. Your handicap may be in reading or speech. If your parents are divorcing, that's a handicap. No matter what you're facing, I just ask you to do one thing, and that's to do the best you can with what you've got."

Some people who see handicaps in others find a reason to turn away. But being vulnerable to others' pain is part of giving. Several years ago, Pat went to Inchon, South Korea, with the hope of teaching English to Korean children set to be adopted. What she found horrified her. "One morning a Korean man walked in with three daughters, ages two, four, and six. Though I could not speak the language, I knew what was going on. He had come to give his daughters away. He and his wife were ashamed that they had had six girls. In Korea, as in all of Asia, girls cannot carry on the family name, so they are considered almost worthless. I was staggered by this blatant devaluation of human life."

Anyone who risks being touched by cruelty and injustice also risks being touched by joy. Several years after Korea, Pat found herself in the bushlands of Zaire as part of a four-week mission trip. They might as well have been her own students, because Pat wouldn't allow differences to stand in the way of compassion. "These kids thought I was strange," she recalls, laughing. "They didn't know what to do with a blue-eyed, white-skinned woman. But one more day and I would have won them over.

"I realized I was a missionary, a missionary with clay feet. We all have weaknesses, and the amazing thing is that God used my weaknesses, my handicaps, to do the work of the kingdom. God works through our own brokenness." That's how Pat Chaney is changing her world with each Lydia that walks into her life.

Years earlier, Pat could have become bitter toward God because her niece was handicapped. She could have politely declined the opportunity to help the multihandicapped children across the street from her own school. She could have looked at her responsibilities to her niece and her own students and said, "God, I can't do one more thing. I can't give any more of myself to anyone." But, like Roger, Pat discovered that human limitations can be a gift. Pat's initial inadequacy to understand what good could come from her niece's handicap became a blessing. In her cries of "Why God?" she deepened a lifelong dialogue with the Lord she loves and serves.

People like Roger and Pat have taught me that love is greater than one's sense of inadequacy or handicap. They have taught me that the place at which you're vulnerable, the place at which you say "I can't," is where impossible beginnings take place. If you ever doubt this can be true for yourself, just ask a couple who live in southern Pennsylvania. Look back more than thirty years ago and you will see a snapshot of two people who refused to say "I can't."

In the spring of 1964, Jim and Mae Teeter were enjoying their family. They could look out through the living room window of their home in Waynesboro and see acres of maple and pine trees that covered the foothills of the nearby Blue Ridge Mountains. Jim Teeter loved this view.

"This land is going to be a wonderful place for the boys, a safe haven away from the danger and trouble of the city," he said to himself.

Their new home quickly became a magnet for ongoing hospitality and special occasions. Like the morning Mae cooked breakfast for thirty missionaries who were leaving for overseas. Libby, the family's baby-sitter, couldn't stand by and watch. "You need someone to help you," she told Mae. "You need someone to watch Mark. He may only be three years old, but he's shown me more love in those three years than I've received all my life." Mae and Jim knew what she meant. Maybe it was his unusual degree of affection. Or the disarming innocence. Jim had lost his patience with Mark one morning at breakfast, saying, "Don't throw your eggs on the floor, son."

"I didn't throw them, Dad," Mark answered. "They just fell that way."

Or maybe what made him special was the way he prayed so many times before bed, "Dear God, help Mommy and Daddy on the mission field." He knew his parents had been planning for months to go to the Ivory Coast in western Africa. It would be a short-term trip during which Jim could use his skills as a surgeon to help people who had never seen a doctor.

The weeks leading up to the trip, however, had not been kind. On New Year's Eve, a fire partially destroyed the Teeters' home. Two months later, Jim and Mae miraculously survived a car crash outside of Baltimore. Then in April, their oldest son Timothy, who had suffered from scarlet fever, became seriously ill with rheumatic carditis and borderline heart failure.

The Teeters were ready to put all of this behind them

and get on with their lives. On April 22, the sun was out and all four boys—Paul, Timothy, John, and three-year-old Mark—were riding their bicycles in the driveway. The far end of the oval loop was a safe distance from the two-lane county road that ran past the house. There was lots of shouting that morning, claims of who could go the fastest and who could turn the quickest. The shouting stopped when Timothy heard a car door slam. Somehow, without even looking up, he sensed what had happened. He shouted just one word.

"Mark!"

Mae ran out of the kitchen. At the end of the driveway, she saw an upturned tricycle. Her three-year-old son lay on the pavement. With his brothers standing silently nearby, she tried to find a pulse. There was none. A man she couldn't identify volunteered to drive her and Mark to the hospital. Minutes later the boy was spread out on an examining table. Someone had phoned Jim Teeter. Now, he was breathing into his son's mouth, trying to revive his little heart. Again and again he tried. Still, there was no response. Sometime around 11:20 that morning, the Teeters' world came to a stop. They had lost their best prayer partner in the world, their youngest child, their Mark.

"I was so grief-stricken I thought surely I would die," recalls Jim. "I wondered if I wanted to keep on living." For months he punished himself for not being able to save his son's life. Somehow Jim and Mae Teeter and their three surviving sons got through the next week. And two months later, still carrying a weight too heavy to bear, Jim and Mae Teeter fulfilled their dream of traveling to the Ivory Coast. They did not realize it was only the beginning. At least once during each of the next thirty years, they would go to a place of need somewhere in the world—Pakistan, Taiwan, Ethiopia, and India—to serve, to operate on sick patients, to comfort, and to tell others about the God in whose name they had come.

When the Teeters returned to Waynesboro, the maple trees that Mark had helped his father plant as a child were a little bit taller. Jim Teeter looked out over the twenty-five acres he had thought about preserving for his boys. Only now he saw the fields his son would never know being enjoyed by other children. All the place needed was a name. The next spring, Mark Victor Teeter Memorial Park was dedicated as a summer camp for Child Evangelism Fellowship. A busload of boys and girls from eight to twelve years old came and learned how they were deeply loved by God.

Since that summer in 1964, more than 12,000 children have come to the field and inner tubed down the east branch of the Little Antietam Creek that supplies water for the pond. Many have returned year after year as campers. Some have come back as junior counselors and as parents bringing their own children. Today, some of the first campers are missionaries serving around the world. They can trace what they're doing today to the week they spent on twenty-five acres in southern Pennsylvania—to a place that was created because a mother and father who lost their son when he was just three years old decided to give out of their loss so that other children could hear about the One they call Jesus, who takes special delight in children.

Jim and Mae Teeter were in their mid-thirties when they said good-bye to Mark. At the time of their greatest loss, their best years still lay ahead of them. They could have held on to their country home, retreated, and lived comfortably. But they chose to do the opposite. They chose to give their lives away. Even if they wanted to, they could not stop the dream they planted long ago. Long after they are gone from this earth, the maples will still be growing, the stream will still be flowing, and the children will still be arriving every summer. That's the way love works, especially when "the rest of your life" is still before you. Especially while you still have the time to take another look at the choice that seems too overwhelming, too demanding, and perhaps too right to ignore.

When was the last time you faced an impossible situation, and said to yourself:

- "The challenge seems so overwhelming, I can't try"?
- "The sacrifice seems so costly, I can't continue"?
- "The loss seems so total, I can't recover"?

Before you turn the page . . .

- The challenge that comes with trying
- The sacrifice that comes with giving
- The loss that comes with risking oneself

When was the last time one of these three consequences caused you to say "I can't"?

Look at your second piece of paper, "What will I do with the rest of my life?" Do you find yourself saying "I can't" to any of your specific hopes and dreams? If so, which ones? What specific challenge, sacrifice, or potential loss are you afraid of making? If you're having trouble coming up with anything, it may be that you live more of your life at the other end of the spectrum. One hundred and eighty degrees from "I can't" is another stifling approach to life so potentially injurious, so deserving of our attention, it's the heart of chapter 5.

CHAPTER FIVE

The Moment You Realize Your Life Is a Runaway Train . . .

A true story: A woman whose husband of many years had just died decided to place an obituary in *The New York Times*. She knew that George had made so many friends over the years, it would be impossible to write them all. So, she phoned the newspaper and asked the representative for the least expensive rate for such a listing. To keep costs down, she indicated to him that the obituary need read only, "George died."

The *Times* representative dutifully typed the two words on his keyboard then said to the woman, "This minimum listing price allows you to use five words, ma'am. Would you like to say anything else?"

The woman thought again. "Yes," she said, "add the words, 'Buick for Sale.'"

Are you laughing or crying? Perhaps you are feeling like doing a little of both. Your life, and mine, will be summed up one day in a handful of words for friends and loved ones to read. If you want an accurate picture of the world you live in, look past the front-page headlines and read the obituaries. There you will see what people did during their short time on earth, where they lived, how they spent their lives. And how they'll be remembered.

How a person leaves this earth says a lot about how he or she lived. In the fall of 1978, saying farewell was the last thing on my mind. I couldn't die; I was too busy. I had too much going on, too much left to accomplish. By the time I was forty-five years old, I considered myself successful by any definition of the word. I was

- chief of staff at the hospital where I did most of my work,
- a member of the hospital's Board of Trustees, and
- the soon-to-be president of the California State Neurosurgical Society.

Every day was one more adrenaline rush. My appointment book was bulging and getting fuller with every phone call. Patients were waiting as much as six weeks just for a consultation. Then there were the surgeries. Sometimes three or four brain or spinal operations a day, and usually at least eight each week. Scheduling went into nights and weekends. Some of these operations were twelve or more hours long. Plus, I was booking elective cases weeks ahead.

Every physician referral, every patient whose life hung in the balance, and every colleague who asked my opinion made me feel so important I couldn't say no. Even though I was killing myself. When it wasn't a scheduled operation, it was a phone call from the emergency room. One unforgettable Sunday afternoon, two motorcycle gangs had a "rumble." The emergency room was filled with the riders who had been beaten on the head with beer bottles and motorcycle chains. I must have examined a dozen of these bloodied men and did brain operations on three.

At 2:30 A.M., I finally finished the last operation and made it home to bed. Fifteen minutes later the phone rang. "This is the emergency room, we need you right away. They've just brought in another victim. He's got a knife sticking in his back and is partially paralyzed with a spinal cord injury." It was 7:00 A.M. and after nearly twelve hours of surgery—with only a fifteen-minute break for sleep—I finally placed the last stitch in the patient's skin. In the operating theater across the hall I could see the nurses positioning my 7:30 A.M. surgery patient on the operating table. After a quick cup of coffee, it was time to start another day.

That evening I fell back into my favorite chair. At that moment I felt sure that I would never be able to stand on my feet again. Every muscle ached, and I felt terribly fatigued. Praying that the telephone wouldn't ring again, I picked up the evening newspaper. I read the front page, glanced through the sports, then flipped to the back page. Under the weather map and local forecast, right next to each other like ironic bookends on life's mantel, were the birth announcements and the obituaries.

My eyes went to the photograph of a middle-aged man, like me. The words that described his life indicated he had died of a heart attack. As I stared at the print, the obituary began to blur, and I began to wonder if the next day's paper might have my photograph, and my life's story, and all that I had accomplished reduced to one-third of a column of newsprint.

Some people ask the question, "What am I going to do with the rest of my life?" then balk at what the answer could mean. Their response to challenges, possibilities, and doing what they really want to do is "I can't." These words didn't exist in my dictionary. I knew exactly what I was going to do and how I was going to get there. The only problem was that it almost cost me my health.

Where are you on the continuum between "I can't do this" and "I'll do it, or else"? Does your life feel like it's going around a mountaintop turn at seventy miles an hour? "Not *me*," you say, "but I know someone who *is*." Regardless of whether this chapter is a mirror for yourself, a spouse, or a friend, I want you to know I'm really writing to myself. Though I've not walked in your moccasins, I've known what it's like to tumble toward the edge where there is no guardrail. Let me tell you what I saw.

At some moment of perspiration and stress, you and I have asked, "How did I get myself into this?" This question comes in varying shades of panic depending upon your age and how much you chose to bite off. It could have been that first, terrifying glimpse of a blind date, volunteering for PTA, or riding the Rock-o-Plane with a child who's just eaten a week's worth of cotton candy, hot dogs, and pop. The risk factor in all three is equally frightening. When we're young, life seems more forgiving. Dad bails you out of the paper route you forgot to do. Instead of suffering the failing grade, the teacher lets you take a make-up exam. After all you had the flu.

But somewhere along the way, the rules stiffen. You're not just responsible for handing in homework anymore. There are people waiting for you at work on Monday morning. They've invested time and money in you. People are counting on you—the manager you don't click with, the elderly parent who's asked you for a ride, the hungry, crying infant who doesn't care that it's 3:30 A.M. Your initiation rite into American adulthood came the day you joined forces with someone else—a spouse, a business partner, a boss. That's when your identity, your choices— the decisions that shape your life—became tied to others, when the word "me" drifted into something called "we."

Which brings us to where you're sitting, right now. Within this past week, perhaps even today, you may have felt you were in over your head, wondering what to do next about a big decision. I don't know what you're facing, but I am quite sure of one thing: the choice about this matter, just like your choice about what to do with the rest of your life, will probably be shaped by two things:

- Trusting a person who helps you

- Seizing a promising opportunity

Think, again, of the big decision that may be looming on the horizon or already sitting in your lap. Instead of letting it overwhelm you (as you may have already experienced), hold it comfortably in your hands as you read on and as you consider the person and the opportunity God may be preparing. It may not be entirely clear what He's doing. I know from personal experience.

When I was thirty-three years old, I was waking up at five-thirty every morning. After a hurried breakfast of cold cereal and black coffee, I made a brisk walk to the University Medical Center two blocks away. When I finished my residency training a few months later, I knew I'd be practicing neurosurgery in Ventura, California. The patients would contact me and drive to my office. Later, some would enter the hospital for surgery. After the operation, I would go up and down the hospital corridors making rounds on all my patients. Easy, quick, and rewarding—just how we want life to work out.

But in 1967 the field of neurosurgery and the farmlands of Ventura County were still relatively young. Neurosurgery had come into its own after World War II. Treating the masses of war wounded had brought about exciting progress in operating on the brain and spinal cord. This kind of surgery—which had once been nonexistent, or at least limited to major university hospital centers—had come to places like the one I was ready to call home.

Ventura was a small seaside town of fifty thousand people, though nearby Oxnard and a dozen smaller towns in the county brought the total population to a half-million. With this many people, a neurosurgeon was badly needed by the time one finally arrived in 1959. His name was Dr. William J. James. He didn't think it was right for patients with brain and spinal problems to have to drive twenty, thirty, fifty or more miles to see a neurosurgeon. One morning we were striding across the parking lot to his car, heading off to do a brain tumor operation at a nearby state mental hospital. "Boy [being from St. Louis, he always called me this], let me tell you now, you have to go where the people are. A brain tumor doesn't pay any attention to where a person lives or how far they have to drive to a hospital or how much money they're forced to live on. Why should we treat people with any less attention? Do you hear what I'm telling you?"

Because of his commitment to serve others, Bill James was the reason I was rolling through the Santa Clara Valley at 4:00 A.M. with my neurosurgical instruments nestled in a worn, black doctor's bag in the back seat. Bill James was the reason why after completing that morning's emergency operation in an outlying community hospital, I would operate in two other large hospitals in separate cities before lunchtime.

Bill James was the reason why I had to change the oil regularly in my car.

Bill James was the reason why thousands of fathers and mothers, children and uncles, business leaders and out-of-work people with no means to pay were able to receive neurosurgical care when they needed it. Because of what he did for them and what he did for me, Bill James was much of the reason why I was able to build a highly successful career in medicine.

Before I knew what it was like to really seek after and follow God, He brought many people into my life as models of compassion, integrity, and trust. Dr. Bill James was one of those people. In the midst of my runaway ambition, in the frantic, professional chaos of trying to make it, God was already at work. In the midst of my growing discontent, God helped me seize a promising opportunity through the gift of a trusting person who had my best interests in mind. Years before I got around to asking the question, Bill James was already showing me the answer. From the moment I met him he was larger than life. His graying red hair and ruddy complexion were unavoidable. So were the questions he put to me in our first interview.

"How did you happen to decide to become a doctor?" "What led you to go into neurosurgery?" "Why are you giving up an opportunity to stay on the medical school faculty in order to practice neurosurgery here in the country?"

Then, looking me squarely in the eye, he made this

statement. "If you want a good place to live and raise your kiddies, a place where you can help take care of some very nice people, then we would love to have you join us. You won't make a lot of money, but making money isn't our calling in becoming doctors. It's offering care to people who need it."

The questions revealed an endearing quality about the man with whom I would work for the next eighteen years. He had grown up in Rhode Island, the son of a navy man. At twenty he joined the merchant marine. Like so many of his generation who were raised in the Great Depression, he bankrolled his future on a priceless resource called desire. After college he graduated from St. Louis University Medical School. When the world changed forever with the bombing of Pearl Harbor on an innocent Sunday morning, December 7, 1941, Bill James found himself an officer in the United States Navy. He served as the chief of surgery on board the *USS Randolph*, an aircraft carrier steaming through the dangerous waters of the South Pacific.

He was thirty when he entered the navy as a junior lieutenant. Just thirteen years later, he wore the four gold stripes and the silver star of a rear admiral. Along the way Bill James completed residency training at the Lahey Clinic in Boston. Then he leapfrogged his way to the top of his field and was named chief of neurosurgery at Balboa Naval Hospital in San Diego.

When you make it to the top of the heap like this man did, where do you go from there? What do you do with the rest of your life?

Bill James made the unlikely choice. He could have spent the next twenty years as an admiral in the navy. He could have spent the rest of his life in modest comfort and prestige. But one day, much to the surprise of his uniformed peers, he traded in his admiral's stripes for a road map of Ventura County, where there were people who had no neurosurgeon. It meant leaving his wife, Elsa, and their two children in San Diego for the first six months. It meant driving to every hospital within a twenty-five-mile radius and making his lifesaving specialty available where and when it was needed.

By the time I met him, eight years after he had settled in Ventura, Bill James had developed a neurosurgical practice that caused him to literally run from patient to patient and race from hospital to hospital. His medical sojourn was a daily exercise in caring, going to the *patient's* hospital, driving up to twenty miles to perform each surgery. He added a partner, Dr. Paul Karlsberg, but it was not enough to meet the demand of people in need.

For at least the first six months, I was in awe of "the Admiral, Doctor William J. James." He repeatedly asked me to call him "Bill." My usual response: "Okay, Dr. James." I simply admired this man so much that "Bill" wasn't a word that came easily. It was a thrill to assist him in surgery and to have him help on my cases. Sometimes when I was deep inside a brain tumor, doing delicate surgery and fighting bleeding that was difficult to control, he would say, "Boy, hang in there, God hates a coward!"

In the operating room, Bill James's skill was obvious. He also did a poor job disguising his compassion. Growing up during the Great Depression gave him compassion for the poor, the sick, and the hurting. It's what led him to work as a ship's steward in order to earn the money needed for medical school. He remembered the day in 1945 when a twin-engine Japanese bomber loaded with two 500-lb.

bombs eluded the radar and intentionally crashed into the starboard flight deck of the *Randolph*. The massive explosion and the fire that followed left 26 dead, 3 missing, and 105 wounded. It also left Bill James, the doctor who treated the wounded and the dying, with memories of suffering he would never forget.

"My kid brother was captured by the enemy at Corregidor. He was a part of that death march at Bataan. My mama sent frequent packages to him through the Red Cross. We found out later that long after he had starved to death, the enemy was still accepting those food parcels." As he told this story, tears would come to his eyes.

This was the admiral who had known the privileges of rank and considered it a privilege simply to treat others with respect and dignity. When it came to giving himself to others, Bill James just couldn't help himself.

Being available. The willingness to go anywhere at any time not because you have to, but because it's the right thing to do. This kind of spontaneous generosity was Bill James's signature on life. He had left a world of reputation and relative comfort because something inside said, "Go, risk yourself and complete the unfinished desire of your heart."

As one who felt the risk of building a new career in a new land, I didn't know how much I needed a Bill James. I didn't know how intoxicating the prestige and power of medicine could be. I didn't know the lure of money could cause even the most well-intentioned physician to view a patient as a potential income source. I didn't know how much the character of one man could lift me beyond these temptations and remind me of what life is really all about.

In our fifth year of partnership, our practice list had

tripled since the days of linoleum and worn shag carpeting on the floor. The load became so heavy, the patient decisions so intertwined, we could function only as a team. That's when I saw the real mentor in Bill come out. Day or night, if I had a difficult decision to make or a demanding emergency operation to do, he would be at my side in minutes. No matter what the hour, when I telephoned him the phone rang only once.

It's one thing to take advantage of a person. It's quite another to call someone on a moment's notice because you would do the same for that person. That's how unconditional giving bred mutual trust. As he continued practicing in his mid-sixties, and his pace began to slow, I found myself doing more and more of the difficult cases he didn't feel he could do any longer. But he still loved to assist me, day or night.

One such emergency case was particularly memorable. At two o'clock in the morning, I telephoned Bill to tell him I had a patient with a severe head injury requiring immediate surgery. "I'll be right there," he said. Click.

An hour must have gone by, and I was well into the operation, working with help from the surgery resident. There was no Bill James. I began to wonder if he had rolled over and gone back to sleep. At that moment the doors of the operating room swung open. A stocky figure with his face flushed and his surgical cap cockeyed on his head thundered in. "What are you trying to do, Boy? Why didn't you tell me you were here at County Hospital? Went all the way to St. Johnnie's in Oxnard, and their operating rooms over there were as quiet as a church!"

"I'm sorry, Bill, but you hung up the telephone before I could tell you where I was operating."

My apology reached him just as he was going through the door into the scrub room to wash his hands. Poking his head back through the door, this time it was the *admiral* who spoke.

"Don't call me Bill, Boy! It's Dr. James." He disappeared again. After several seconds he pushed the scrub room door open again, this time with his foot. "In fact, it's Admiral James, Admiral James, *sir*!"

It was all I could do to keep from laughing. Inside his burly frame, the same spark that ignited a hot temper fueled this bighearted man. He was different from so many other neurosurgeons I had met who tended to be self-absorbed, confident, and overbearing. One day I came back to the office and learned there was a plumbing leak in the tank of our only toilet. The receptionist whispered through a grin, "You won't believe who's fixing it."

I had to see for myself. Here was the admiral, sitting backward on the toilet, sleeves rolled up and shirttail out. He had one arm inside the tank and the other arm sticking through the porcelain bottom. His sweaty face was pressed against the tank's grimy edge as he fought to twist a stubborn nut onto a rusted bolt.

"I can't talk to you now, Boy. I'm busier than a one-armed paperhanger."

I thought of asking him why he hadn't simply called a plumber. But I already knew the answer. Bill would do anything he could to keep our overhead down and our patient fees down in the process. Seeing the former navy admiral and gifted physician straddling a broken toilet said it all: When a part of life didn't work the way God intended—whether it was the human brain or a toilet—this man did everything in his power to fix it. On that day

Bill James gave the word *neurosurgeon* a new synonym: servant.

The frustrating beauty of a person like Bill is that he didn't know how to quit. What motivated him to give to others also kept him from giving up, even if it meant failing to take a well-deserved vacation. Each year he would say something like, "Elsa and I are going to Europe. Always wanted to go over there and see the sights. Looking forward to getting away." But the time never came. The travel dates always got buried and forgotten under a new stack of appointment sheets. He may as well have tried vacationing on Saturn. The idea of relaxing just wasn't in his universe.

After twenty years of postponements, Bill and Elsa made the trip. When he came home, I realized how far Bill had grown up from the culture of France.

Bill on famous Paris art museums: "I do remember being in the Lu-vor, but that's about all."

Bill on memorable rail destinations in Austria: "We got on some train, but I'll tell you I don't know where we went." Quickly changing the subject he said, "Boy, I'll tell you what I *do* remember and that is I have X rays on several patients that I want you to look at with me. Come on, we've got work to do."

The vacation was over. We were on the fast track again. That night after staying too late at the office again, I came home to face a warmed-up dinner, too tense, too tired to look up.

"We got on some train, but I'll tell you I don't know where we went."

Bill James's train ride was my harried reality. Somewhere between my first early morning surgical expeditions and the larger practice we had "succeeded" in building, I had climbed aboard a runaway train. For the first time in my life, I admitted to myself that my career was out of control. For the first time in my professional life, I felt scared.

Its popular name is "midlife crisis." But you don't have to be between the ages of thirty-five and fifty to be convinced its impact is frightening and harsh: The things you always believed in—your company, your abilities, your goals—suddenly lose their meaning when the years of expectation don't live up to their promise. As a boy, I remember seeing the big, bold words on the outside of a box of breakfast cereal: "Giant U.S. Navy PT Boat, Only 25 Cents!" The back of the box was dominated by a picture of a massive U.S. attack boat. "Watch it sail through the water as you create your own secret mission!" This wasn't a toy for the bathtub. This was an armament so massive that it demanded "four to six weeks for delivery." The waiting period seemed almost unbearable. For the next month, the empty cereal box—minus the side flap I had cut out and mailed along with a quarter—sat on my dresser like a monument.

Finally, my long-awaited, U.S. Navy PT boat arrived at our house on the prairie. Its huge container was a cardboard box, six inches long. I pulled out my gray, wooden dream. It was just slightly bigger than one of my father's ink pens. That night in the bathtub, thanks to a teaspoon of baking soda my mother put into its removable top, the PT boat bobbed up and down a few times then came to rest on the bottom of the tub, an unfulfilled promise, a sunken dream.

"What did you expect for twenty-five cents?" said my mother.

What special offer have you looked forward to receiving? What have you been working and saving and going after for years? What's been your dream, your destination, your goal? Does it look the same today as when you first said to yourself, "That's what I'm going after, *that's* what I want"? Or have you had serious doubts lately about where you're headed and what it's taking to get there? If you're too old to be called one of the young alumni by your college, and yet too young to receive the 10 percent senior citizen discount at your favorite restaurant, then you may be feeling the aftershocks from one or more of life's unpleasant midlife tremors:

- You've lost a job. Downsizing, restructuring, or an unfortunate turn of events has forced you to reevaluate your career, question your abilities, and realize that only a limited number of years remain.

- You've faced a major health problem. The body you took for granted is actually fragile and (gasp!) wearing out.

- You've experienced a painful separation or divorce. This fracture has shaken up everything—relationships, finances, self-confidence, and faith.

- You've lost a spouse or other loved one. His or her death has reminded you of your own.

Sooner or later, one of the above scenarios is going to shift from fiction to autobiography. Sooner or later, we are all humbled by the 85 percent of life that's out of our control, as well as the 15 percent we *think* we can control. What made my crisis so real—to the point that I could no longer avoid the question—was that I was 100 percent sure I didn't like where I was going.

By the time I was fifty, feeling so empty in my success, I had every reason to feel scared. I began to dwell upon the physician's words I had heard nearly twenty years before: "The tests show that your cholesterol is very high. People with this problem usually die early, certainly by middle age." Since that time, I had done all the right things to bring my cholesterol down to the normal range. Now, at age fifty, what really worried me was that I could no longer keep up the pace of seventy-, eighty-, and ninety-hour work weeks. I felt sure it was just a matter of time until I had a heart attack. Let me tell you what convinced me.

When Bill James described his European rail trip, he told of all he had seen in France, Switzerland, and Austria: vast green farmlands and hillsides covered with vineyards, towering snow-covered mountains, with forested alpine meadows and lakes in valleys below. As he talked of speeding through this beautiful countryside on a first-class, fast-moving train, not really knowing where he was heading, Bill gave me a haunting symbol for my life and career. Perhaps you'll be able to relate.

All the years of status climbing, title earning, money making, and name building had given me a first-class seat aboard a comfortable train. There was only one problem. By the time I was fifty, the train had picked up so much speed, I was panicked beyond words. At a time in life when I should have been experiencing and appreciating the passengers and the view God had blessed me with, I found myself trapped on a runaway train that had no clear destination, no conductor—and no brakes.

Each time I've shared this image of life that's dangerously out of control, the other person immediately becomes quiet. He or she then gives me this uncomfortable look that says, "What you're saying hits too close to home. *I'm* on that train, and I want to get off." Frankly, these silent stares of angst and the long conversations that usually follow have convinced me the runaway train is a metaphor for our times.

The train image has personal meaning, because as the son of a railroad travel agent, I had grown up with switching yards and train schedules, always watching the face of the clock to make sure every detail of life stayed on time. During the summers between my years in college and medical school, I worked as a tour director. For three months each year, I would travel from one end of the United States and Canada to the other, then back again six times over. Out of these experiences the train metaphor emerged a living illustration—one that may explain the apprehension, frustration, and helplessness you may feel right now about where your life is headed.

If you're like thousands of Americans who feel their lives are already out of control, you may already be experiencing the first four of these stages. And depending on the choices you've already made, you may be facing the fifth and most disturbing stage. Here are the five stages most of us go through as we travel through life. They're also the five reasons why you might feel you're riding a runaway train and why it seems there's no way to get off.

1. *Making Plans*

In my five summers of leading tour groups by train, I never met a person who had packed his bags by chance. These people were charged and ready to go because they had planned their trip weeks, sometimes months in advance. Now, they were ready to take the long-awaited journey.

What about *your* journey? Imagine you had to design a brochure that described where you're now headed in life. What would your trip look like?

- Where do you want to end up? How would you describe the setting, the lifestyle, the rewards of where you want to be five, ten, twenty years from now?

- How do you plan to get there?

- Are you traveling alone or with someone else?

- What do you expect to see and do along the way?

- What's the one thing you absolutely don't want to miss on your journey?

As you began to plan where you've wanted to go with your life, you notice something is missing in the brochure.

2. *Counting the Cost*

The brochure doesn't mention price. It just talks about the fantastic things you're going to see and do on the trip. As you decide where you want to go in life, and think about all you'd like to see and do, how much have you been willing to spend in terms of time, training, money, or other material sacrifices? Which of these things have you been willing to give up to get where you're going?

Whether you realize it or not, you started your journey with a set price in mind. Somewhere you decided you wanted to "spend" only so much time, effort, sacrifice, and, yes, money, for the trip ahead. This allowed you to take the next step.

3. *Starting Out*

In the brochure you liked the place you were headed and how you planned to get there. Naturally, you wanted a window seat so you could see where you were going. You looked forward to your destination, but you also wanted to enjoy the scenery.

- During the past months and years of your life's journey, what's happened to your original destination, your goal?

- Do you still look forward to arriving there? If so, why? If not, why?

- When you started out, what "scenery" did you experience out your window? Did it live up to the pictures in the brochure?

- Early on, how would you have described the trip? Smooth? A little bumpy at times? What is the ride like today?

- Now that you've been "riding" for a while, what things have made the trip worthwhile? Have you ever wanted to get off?

Maybe you've sat on a real train that's about ready to leave the station. You dozed off for a moment, then opened your eyes and noticed the train was moving. The same thing is true when a train begins to pick up speed.

4. *Going Faster and Faster*

The brochure promised you'd "enjoy your long-awaited journey at a comfortable pace." It didn't say that your train, your life, would begin to race out of control. Is this why you're feeling a bit uncomfortable?

- When did the train—the job, the schedule, the obligations, and demands you're trying to meet— begin to move faster?

- When did you stop paying attention to the scenery and start becoming more concerned about the safety of the train, the condition of the tracks and the concerned looks of the family members, colleagues, and friends who felt trapped on the same train?

- Did you ever stop and ask yourself, "Who's driving this thing? Who or what is running my life?"

Sometimes, as a tour director, I would look out the window and notice we were passing cars being driven on the highway. It was then that I realized the awesome power and force of the machine I was on. And how impossible it would be to stop a 1,000-ton locomotive.

5. *Wanting Off*

In five summers as a tour director, there were a few split seconds when I thought the train we were riding might have been out of control. I can't describe the fear I felt. It wasn't so much a fear of *dying*, it was the fear that in *that* instant there was nothing I could do to escape or change my situation. It was the fear of knowing I was in danger and that everything was out of my control.

I hope your life, your work, and your cherished relationships have not come to this fifth stage. If you've read this far, however, I can only guess that the train you're riding may be dangerously close to jumping the tracks and that you want off. If that's indeed the case, you have cause for warning—and a reason to be glad—because your awareness has taken you through these four levels of progressive understanding:

Unconsciousness. As the pace of life increases, most people react more impulsively and choose less wisely. They push through, unaware and unfazed by life's forces and predicaments.

Denial. Seeing but not wanting to face reality, these people know the train is speeding up, but they'd rather not check it out, so they don't do anything about it. After all, life is better spent looking at the scenery even if it's racing by too fast to really enjoy.

Awareness. These people know for a fact that something's wrong. Maybe they've even pinpointed the problem. They take temporary comfort in knowing what needs to be fixed. But they don't know if it's worth the effort, or worse yet, if life's problems can be answered.

If you're conscious of your life, if you're willing to face reality, if you're aware that something's not quite right, and you believe that God is able to come and meet you in your present condition, then you can know that you weren't created to live life out of control. Then you can live beyond the next treacherous turn.

Hope. While the train has certainly picked up speed, while you live with possible regrets about where and how you've chosen to travel, you meet some fellow passengers who are not at all worried. Though they feel the same bumps and rumbles you do, they are confident of their safe journey and ultimate destination. In fact, their very presence gives you hope that even if your life has indeed become a runaway train, you can actually choose a new destination that gives new and unexpected meaning to your journey, your life.

Between the time I was forty-five and fifty-five I did just that. I moved from blind unawareness of how my career was crumbling to genuine hope for what my life could be. I saw the uncomfortable dilemma that came with a rushed, disconnected, discontented life. By the time I realized the train was picking up speed, it was going too fast for me to get off. The double whammy was that the faster I whizzed towards success, the fewer miles remained. There simply wasn't enough time to do everything. I wanted to spend time with my family and friends. I wanted to travel and listen to classical music and read articles and books. I wanted to reflect about life. Most of all, I wanted to spend the rest of my life making a difference in the lives of others.

Something had to change. Either I could keep up the frenetic pace and risk a coronary, or I could do the impossible. Along the way I had passed some amazing scenery. Fellow passengers like Roger Youmans had helped me see this amazing scenery as opportunities I would never have the chance to explore unless I did the unthinkable—find someone who could stop the train so I could get off and chart a new destination.

As I suggested earlier, the man who helped me to do just this was someone with whom I'd been riding for years. The man who helped me stop the train by helping me see what I could do differently—*even while we worked together at a breakneck speed*—was my mentor and friend, Bill James.

"What are you going to do, Boy?" he would ask me. "Are you going to slow down and take care of yourself and live long enough to enjoy being with your sweetie and your kiddies? Or, are you going to burn yourself out and finally work yourself to death? You just think about what I'm telling you!"

There was nothing synthetic, nothing artificial in the fabric of Bill James. He was made out of 100 percent compassion, a believer who walked with the Lord, who said to me many times, "The knees of my trousers are shiny and nearly worn through just from kneeling down and thanking God for His blessings and asking for His help in taking care of my patients."

It was hard to see the years bring the inevitable changes of advancing age to bear upon this giant of a man. The day finally came when Bill James had to retire from his active neurosurgical practice. Even then he continued to see the poor in the County Hospital Outpatient Clinic and serve on the Community Hospital Board of Trustees. Wherever he went he shared his ready smile and a warm handshake with everybody he met.

Eventually he was able to move about only in a wheelchair. Still, I never heard Bill James complain. He only gave thanks. Even the night after a dinner party when my three younger partners and I lifted Bill from his wheelchair into a car, he displayed the dignity of an admiral and the humility of a child.

On December 29, 1992, the sanctuary of Sacred Heart Church became the most coveted gathering place in Ventura. That morning, as I stood up to deliver the eulogy for Bill James, I looked out and saw the legacy of one man's life, the many men and women who had been his friends and his patients. Many of their lives had been saved by the skillful hands of the surgeon whose flag-draped coffin now rested in front of the altar. They came on crutches or with canes, some in wheelchairs. They sat together in the back pews, many not realizing the ironic way they were related through one man.

Here was the admiral, the man so many had saluted in an earlier life. Now those whom he had loved had gathered to salute him. Now they were giving back to their doctor, their colleague, and their friend the same respect Bill James had given to them. For years he had gone the extra miles to be their cherished physician. Now he was being welcomed into heaven by the Great Physician, the One whom he had known on his knees in prayer and in the lives of so many he sought to serve.

That morning belonged to Bill James and to anyone else who has ever done what he did—take the unflattering, unpopular path of going where the needy are, not because it's convenient, but because it's right.

That is how one man helped me stop a train: When I looked at the snapshot of Bill James's life, I saw him refuse to give in to the temptation of thinking, "I can do it all." Bill James's prescription for such overzealous and ultimately unsatisfying ambition was to simply know it was enough to give all of himself to the thing in life that needed care and fixing—whether it was a broken plumbing fixture or a hurting patient. So when I thought my most productive years were over, I decided to do the unthinkable—get off the train of ambition and go in another direction.

I thought he and I were the only ones foolish enough to do such a thing. Oh, was I wrong.

Have you ever found yourself aboard a runaway train?

Do you find yourself riding one right now, wishing you could get off?

Before you turn the page . . .

You may find yourself in this situation:

Suppose you're barely holding on to a job, a marriage, or another important relationship—it's a train that's out of control. You wonder how you can avoid crashing. As a last resort, you push your way through all the cars until you finally reach the train conductor's booth. You're just about to see what's out of whack—why the train you're riding has gotten so out of control—when you realize there is one thing you can do to slow down the train or avoid crashing. You grab the microphone for the intercom system. What do you say to the other passengers you find yourself riding with? In other words, what instruction do you need to give *yourself* to slow down the runaway train in your own life?

CHAPTER SIX

The Difference One Person Can Make

I had heard about the book from several friends. The title alone intrigued me: *The Longevity Factor.*[†] Once I began reading, I couldn't put it down.

The statistics that describe this revolution may be familiar to you already. In 1900, the average life expectancy at birth for a newborn baby was roughly 47 years; in 1991, it was about 75 (72 for men and 79.2 for women). That is a net gain of 28 years. Thus, since the turn of the century, the lifetime of the ordinary American has lengthened by 60 percent, and the amount of time that we spend in adulthood has more than doubled. . . .

You may find that your adult life will be twice as long as you think it is going to be. If you have had reasonably good health habits, by the time you celebrate your sixtieth birthday, instead of being on the downward slope of old age you may have two or three decades of productive adult life ahead of you—time that is not much different in quality from what you experience at sixty.

What Lydia Brontë, Ph.D., says in her book affirms what I've seen over the past decade. People in their sixties, seventies, and beyond are discovering that the future they thought would never come has suddenly arrived. After asking themselves, "What will we do after we quit working?" they're realizing that "the rest of our lives" is *now*:

Jerry Miller was always greeted by a mountain of phone messages at work. By the time he was thirty-nine, he had worked his way up to division manager of Texaco Incorporated. He became the youngest man in the country to hold such a top-level executive position with the large oil company. Today, as executive director of the Billy Graham Training Center at The Cove, a Christian conference center, he still returns as many as twenty phone calls a day. For a fraction of the financial remuneration, he and his wife, Dee, began a new career. "We have never for one minute looked back on our decision or had any question concerning having made the correct decision. We feel confident that God has called us to this work, and we give thanks to Him every minute of every day for leading us in this way."

Bob Dennis is seventy-three. He gets up every morning at 6:00. Though his last formal full-time job was twenty-two years ago, he will work four- to twelve-hour days, today, as part of a work team that builds homes for low-income farm workers near his hometown of Cowiche, Washington.

"Building houses for Habitat is hard work. Still, seeing the faces of the people who work alongside me and who will end up living in the house makes it all more than worthwhile. When the job is completed, I always feel that

I am the one who has been blessed the most. It is such a delight working with the variety of people who are involved in helping others. I feel that together we are the hands and feet doing the work of the body of Christ here on earth."

For twenty-seven years as the senior pastor of Community Presbyterian Church in Palm Desert, California, Dean Miller enjoyed bringing people together in Sunday morning worship, weddings, and Bible studies. He tried to retire, but it didn't work. Opportunities for connecting strangers with like interests and dreams kept getting in the way. These meetings have been the catalyst for global missions projects and local outreach efforts that have changed the lives of drug addicts and homeless men and women in his own city.

"Now that I'm 'out of the ministry,'" he says facetiously, "I have all kinds of time to keep on doing what I've always enjoyed doing, putting people together who want to do God's work." He confesses, "When it comes to this chronic habit of matchmaking, I guess I just can't help myself." At age sixty-five, he is still making this confession.

Then there is Aart Van Wingerden, a native of the Netherlands, who came to America with six dollars in his pocket. Over his sixty-five-year career, he has pioneered ways to dramatically increase the size and the growth rate of plants, trees, animal feed, and virtually anything that can benefit from the right balance of sun, water, and ingenuity. Today, this combination has blossomed into a thriving business with markets in ten states and humanitarian projects in four countries abroad. He owns and operates one of the largest greenhouse operations in the

United States, with over thirty-five acres of flowers and plants under roof.

Well into his seventies, he has often said to me, "Mel, I have this problem: I make money. I can't seem to help it. I just do." Aart's "problem" may be genetic. Today, all of his sixteen children are in the greenhouse business. "The kids are my greatest competitors, and I like it that way." The phenomenal business growth that led to the creation of a family nonprofit organization that has helped farmers in Indonesia, Haiti, Honduras, and Ethiopia literally to double their harvests may never have come about had Aart not reached a turning point in his work and his faith at the age of forty-seven.

Aart and Cornelia Van Wingerden—like Jerry and Dee Miller, Dean and Carol Miller, and Bob Dennis—have experienced the joy of giving and the assurance that one person can make a difference despite how "old" he or she is. At a time in life when a lot of people think their lives are almost over, all of these people realized their best years were still before them. The people you'll read about found surprising new meaning, direction, and purpose in their latter years because they were willing to admit the truths we've talked about:

Physical death will come to you someday (chapter 1). You and I face a limited number of years. Is death, for you, the ultimate enemy? Or is it an ally, not a feared foe but a valued friend, that motivates you to ask, "What has made my life meaningful to this point? If I had only ten years of life left, what would I do, and what kind of person would I be?"

Some key motivation, faith, or core belief is driving your life (chapter 2). What has driven your life to this point? Are these the same values that will shape your goals and hopes for the next ten years?

Your decision of what to do with the rest of your life will likely be guided by one or more unforgettable role models (chapter 3). In a world that values *getting,* the people who show us *giving* make us see what life is really all about. The good news is that mentors can come at any age and stage of life.

The human response to the thought of giving ourselves to others is "I can't" (chapter 4). However, it's only one end on the spectrum of how and where we look for meaning in life. The other extreme is equally paralyzing.

The attitude of "I can do it all" can generate so much determination and confidence that our lives become out of control (chapter 5). By the time we realize we're in trouble, it seems there's little we can do but hold on and hope for the best, even when possible life-threatening harm is just around the bend.

These truths brought each of the people you've just met to a critical turning point in life. And these are the truths that bring us to a turning point in this book. Look at your own life. On the spectrum called "Driving Motivation," where would you place yourself between these two extremes?

"What I want out of life (for me) is . . ."

"What I want out of life (for others) is . . ."

On the spectrum called "Attitude and Ambition," where would you place yourself between these two extremes?

"I can't possibly do this."

"I can do it all."

Maybe you aren't sure where you fit on both lines. But when you look at your life, today, you can't avoid the questions:

- Is this how I want to keep living the rest of my life?

- Would I really be happy doing and thinking the same things?

- Is unhappiness, restlessness, or a growing sense of God's presence and call in my life causing me to say, "You can't keep going like this"?

- Does something in my life need to change? If so, what? And if so, how?

By now it may be obvious: As you begin to ask these questions, you're actually "answering" the question, "What will I do with the rest of my life?" There are, of course, no convenient, neatly packaged solutions. Instead there are people, everyday men and women who arrived at their own turning points with few real answers. The word *serendipity* means "an apparent aptitude for making fortunate discoveries accidently." The "fortunate accident" of this chapter is that I had no idea, starting out, that the people in their *midlife* and beyond would so perfectly illustrate how to ask (and answer!) the question at the *midpoint* of this book. It is no accident, however, that each of these people has experienced a life turnaround because of a cherished common conviction that could only come from one source.

Some business leaders meet with their employees in a crowded conference room. When Jerry Miller met with his employees, he usually booked entire hotels or convention centers. As a Texaco executive responsible for all retail marketing in the United States, and later as director of the Human Resource Program for Texaco, USA, Jerry's employee roster hovered right around 20,000. He had never aspired to be one of a hundred high-powered executives that ran one of America's five largest oil corporations. But talent, drive, and twenty-eight years with the same company had a way of elevating one's career.

Why then, at age fifty-five, did he decide to leave it all and go to work for a tiny fraction of his six-figure salary? What made one of Texaco's most powerful leaders turn his back on the privileges of limousine service, free perks in private lunch and country clubs, a six-week company-paid vacation, and incentive compensation plans? What led him to go to work for a fledgling Christian training center for the salary of a Texaco gas station attendant?

One day back in December 1982, Jerry got a call from Robertson McQuilken, president of Columbia Bible College in South Carolina. He wanted to know if Jerry would be willing to head up the operation of a proposed retreat site in Asheville, North Carolina, called The Cove.

"At the time the property had no buildings, no people, no training program, and no roads," recalls Jerry. "These 1,500 acres of heavily wooded mountains and winding valley were nature's backdrop for a vision of Billy and Ruth Graham. They wanted to create a training center for Christian laypeople, a place where Bible teachers could share God's Word. This was the legacy Mr. Graham wanted to leave. In fact, he said, 'As a Christian training center, The Cove will have only one textbook, the Bible.'"

After Jerry finished talking to Robertson McQuilken, he sat down at the kitchen table and shared the opportunity with his wife, Dee. Over the years they had received offers to leave Texaco. But none quite like this. They knew the definition of *relocate* before the word became chic in the mobile, manic decade of the 1980s. In twenty-eight years with Texaco, they had greeted the moving van nineteen times. For some families the centerpiece on their coffee table is a guest book. For the Millers it was a Rand McNally Road Atlas.

Most people, when faced with a big decision, ask, "Why *should* we do this?" Jerry and Dee Miller looked at the opportunity to move away from guaranteed security and comfort, and asked, "Why *shouldn't* we do this?"

It would not be inaccurate, or demeaning, to describe Jerry and Dee Miller's decision-making process as unusual. Make that unusual *and* wise. Says Jerry:

> We've found that over the years, God has spoken to us through His Word, the Bible. I don't mean opening the Bible randomly and pointing to the first verse you see. I mean listening for the Lord to speak through godly people. If someone I didn't know had come up to me at church and said, "Jerry, I think you should leave Texaco and move to The Cove," I would have had a hard time even considering such an offer. How could I trust knowing God's voice without trusting the person's relationship with God?
>
> I knew Robertson McQuilken loved and obeyed God. He is a faithful Christian we have known and served with on the college board for years. Because I knew him, because I trusted his relationship with God, I could trust the invitation to consider coming to The Cove. The invitation also came from Mr. Graham, and I knew I could trust him! They invited Dee and me to consider the offer only after spending weeks in prayer. They were interested in hearing and obeying God. Therefore, considering the invitation of godly individuals was

not an unreasonable thing to do. That's why we believe whenever you face an opportunity that comes from godly men and women interested in doing the Lord's work, it is not unreasonable to believe God already has your best interest in mind; it is not then unreasonable to ask, *"Why shouldn't we do this?"*

Jerry and Dee Miller sat at the kitchen table that night. For the next four hours they talked and prayed. And they decided to write down on a yellow legal pad all of the possible reasons for saying no to the invitation they had received. By the time the evening was over their yellow pad was still blank. Despite having to move for the twentieth time (at their expense), despite giving up a six-figure salary, despite letting go of the wall-to-wall comfort and security of the corporate world, and despite making a job change when most of their friends were making winter vacation plans in Hawaii, Jerry and Dee Miller did the only reasonable thing they could with the rest of their lives. They said yes to opportunity; yes to challenge, sacrifice, and risk; yes to serving others. And, most of all, they said yes to God.

They moved from a spacious home in Houston's high-rent district to a two-bedroom condominium in the mountains of Asheville, North Carolina. It was not the biggest adjustment they had to make. According to Jerry:

> The biggest surprise was learning you can't run a ministry like a business. For the first three or four years it seemed things were moving slowly, but there was never a time in my mind or Dee's that we didn't feel it was going to succeed. Others were not so sure. At The Cove dedication, a couple in town said, "We felt so sorry for you, Jerry, leaving your position with Texaco for this ministry." Deep down, we

believed God had called us to The Cove, and we knew that God is faithful and His timing is perfect, so all we needed to do was be obedient.

After seeing the construction completed, and the programs initiated, Jerry admits wondering whether he should have retired from his position as executive director. "Then, while hearing Dennis Kinlaw speak at a seminar, God spoke to me once again, affirming us in what we were doing. I heard Him say, 'Jerry, serve Jesus here. Forget the "I." You came here because *I* changed your direction in life. You have no right to plan what I'm going to do with the rest of your life.'"

Jerry and Dee did the reasonable thing. They stayed. By the fall of 1994, eleven years after the Millers came to Asheville, The Cove was hosting thirty-six seminars, including a summer camp for kids. Jerry had also responded to the call to take his place on the board of directors of the Billy Graham Evangelistic Association.

"Today, when we drive into The Cove, even though Dee and I have been involved in almost everything from selecting the buildings to selecting the speakers, we feel like we've been spectators. Human beings couldn't do the things we've seen accomplished. It's nothing we've done, it's what God continues to do through ordinary people."

Sometimes the critical turning point in life isn't inspired by changing jobs, but by being out of a job. Sometimes, being out of work is the only way you can land *the opportunity* that allows you to spend the rest of your life doing what you do best. If your name is Dean Miller, you know that being unemployed can be the turning point that frees you to keep giving and keep living your life in the Lord's service.

In 1961 Dean and Carol Miller moved from their home in Oxnard to Palm Desert, California, a small, sun-drenched town southeast of Palm Springs. The residents were a combination of vacationers and retired corporate executives. The Community Presbyterian Church met every Sunday morning in a small church building surrounded by windswept desert. When Dean Miller looked out on the congregation, he saw a handful of people, all pioneers who had carved out a future in untamed acres of sand. During the winter months, he saw the ranks begin to swell, finally reaching several hundred as more and more people came to the desert in search of warm weather.

God had endowed Dean Miller with the special gifts of being a good listener and of being a person who was faithful and worthy of trust. After meeting Dean for the first time, people knew they had a friend. "As the years went by," Dean said, "it just seemed natural to introduce one friend who had a project or a need to another friend who I felt might be able to help."

In 1989, Dean's pastoral duties at Palm Desert Community Presbyterian Church came to an end. "This loss proved to be almost more than I could bear," Dean says, "and I found myself in the deep valley of depression and despair. Then, God's grace lifted me from that valley of dwelling on 'that which I had given up' to the mountaintop experience of focusing on 'that which I *still had to give*.'"

Unemployment can be a cruel wake-up call at any age. For a person in his fifties or sixties, it can be devastating. Dean Miller made it through.

When I said good-bye to the pastorate, I didn't leave behind the gifts God had given to me along the way. For years I didn't really think about bringing people together around a shared interest or need. To me it wasn't work, it was fun. Before long I began to see that whatever talent I had as a minister, God was asking me to use my gifts with people for purposes that were so much greater than what I could ever do by myself. One example of this sits today in the neighboring city of Indio.

It's called the ABC Recovery Center for Addiction. The group was founded by Danny and Helen Leahy out of their battle with alcoholism. Danny wanted to create a home for hurting men and women who could find acceptance, healing, and practical, effective steps to begin a new life free from their addictions. When I met Danny, the center was little more than an old house. There was little or no room for pregnant mothers who came to the center suffering from the effects of alcohol and drugs.

Less than fifteen miles from the center, in Rancho Mirage, lived a man whose company name was known to anyone who has ever bought new tires for a car. I had known Leonard Firestone for years. Because he had a compassionate heart for people in need, I thought he might be interested in the center. He accepted my invitation to come take a look. In the well-worn lunchrooms and lounges of the center, he saw the cruel lessons of chemical dependence in the faces of women whose children would be born addicted to heroin, LSD, and other drugs if nothing was done. After seeing these people, Leonard Firestone decided he wanted to help build a place they could call home. By saying yes to this opportunity, he changed the lives of men and women, drug addicts, he would never meet.

Dean's gift of networking stretched further. He introduced Danny and Helen Leahy to two other influential couples whose lives, like Leonard Firestone, were changed greatly by the ABC Recovery Center for Addiction. Two years after Leonard's first visit to the center, a new wing with living facilities for thirty women was dedicated. It was constructed without a builder's fee by Gordon and Ruth DeWitte, and the original building was expanded to meet the needs of forty-five men. A new restaurant-style kitchen had been installed, thanks to the generosity of Chuck and Maxine Billman. The DeWittes and the Billmans gave more than their money, they gave of themselves by taking places on the center's board of directors. "Sometimes I wonder what would have happened had I never picked up the phone and called Leonard Firestone and the others allowing them to see the need in their own community," Dean said. "I have a feeling that if I hadn't stepped out in faith, God could have easily used someone else to help build the new women's wing."

I like Dean Miller's attitude. I think I know where it comes from.

I don't set out to achieve goals. Instead, I look for people who are open to new opportunities. I call them moments of grace. Most people spend their lives racing along. Their definition of time, accomplishment, and meaning is how long it takes to get from point "a" to point "b." The "time of their life" is *chronos*, the Greek word from which we get *chronology*.

But along this linear race through time, I've continued to meet people who are experiencing another kind of time that's fuller and richer than anything you could measure with an appointment book. This time is called *charis*, or "grace"; from point "a" to point "b" of our lives, God drops in these grace-filled moments. These are the moments strangers warm up to each other over coffee. These are the times when a wealthy businessman decides to invest a part of his earthly fortune in a piece of God's eternal plan that will bring Bibles, electricity, or food to people around the corner or around the world.

If you tend to see the rest of your life as a plan to be defined, measured, and accomplished, consider Dean Miller who tends to value the person rather than the goal. If you happen to forget the ABC Recovery Center for Addiction, one way to remember Dean is to remember one of his former church members who lived in Washington, D.C., but who, in the early 1960s, spent most winters in Palm Desert. The man's name was Dwight Eisenhower.

Dwight Eisenhower taught me the true meaning of greatness. On its cover commemorating the fiftieth anniversary of D Day, *Time* magazine accurately said he was "The Man Who Defeated Hitler." It's incredible to think that this one man was responsible for the critical decision to mobilize 1.5 million troops from twelve allied nations, knowing that the destiny of the free world rested on the success or failure of their predawn invasion.

On Sundays, I would look out on the congregation and see men and women, sitting in the pew next to the general and his wife, Mamie. At home and at work they were losing a daily battle against forces beyond their control. What could I tell them? How could I encourage them in their struggles that seemed impossible to conquer? Without knowing what I was going through, Dwight Eisenhower showed me the answer one day.

We were talking after church one morning. Here was the former president of the United States, the former supreme Allied commander in World War II, reflecting for a moment on his life. I remember him saying that he never really aspired to be president, that he always saw himself as a general in the army. He said he entered the White House with the strong belief that he had been "drafted into public service."

He said he took the office of the presidency seriously, as one should, realizing it was the highest office in the land. Yet he exhibited rare humility in saying he never took himself seriously in the office. I recall him saying that when he was in the Oval Office, he would sit back and laugh at himself and wonder how a farm boy from Kansas could become president of the United States! He said when the pressures came, when they seemed too much to bear, he would lay his head on his pillow before he went to sleep at night and say, "Lord, I've done the best I can. You take over until morning."

In those few words, Dwight Eisenhower made "greatness" synonymous with "humility." In his simple, straightforward prayer, he reminded me that it's only through humility that we receive God's direction and strength.

In a typical month, Dean Miller figures he meets many individuals. For every mountaintop encounter that links one's generosity with another's need there are plenty of others who simply want to talk or to share a concern with a friend who will listen. "Today, my only job description is to use the gifts God has given me," says Dean. "Often, I don't know what, if anything, results from my time with someone else. I just have to go on, like Dwight Eisenhower, and say, 'Lord, I did the best I could, at being the best friend I could be.'"

When you consider your age and the number of years that may still be before you, you could take the attitude of fifty-five-year-old financially secure Jerry Miller and ask, "Why *shouldn't* I do this?"

You could find yourself staring at the future like sixty-year-old, newly out-of-work Dean Miller and ask, "What are the gifts I *can't help* but give to others?"

Or you could look to the future like forty-seven-year-old Aart Van Wingerden, who asked the ultimate question, "What is God calling me to do?"

In 1968, Aart Van Wingerden was a greenhouse operator with ten employees in Carpenteria, California. He and his wife and children had come to America fifteen years before as part of an immigrant group from Holland. In a few short years of hard work, he had built a business which was the envy of local competitors. The Van Wingerdens had established themselves in their new country and had become financially secure and comfortable.

Aart recalls the turning point that forever changed the rest of his life.

A friend at church who was traveling to Chicago one weekend asked me if I would teach his class, "Rich Christians Living in a Needy World." After hesitating somewhat, I said, "Yes, I will." Things went smoothly until I read a verse from 1 John: "But whoever has this world's goods, and sees his brother in need, and shuts up his heart from him, how does the love of God abide in him?" (1 John 3:17). The words were barely out of my mouth when a woman in the group spoke up.

"That's nice, but how do you do what you just said? How do you give to other people's needs?"

I looked at her and said, "I don't know. I'll ask Howie, the real teacher. We'll let him answer it when he is here next week."

"That's not good enough," the woman said. "I can't take a no."

The next day, Howie phoned me and said he was stuck in Chicago; I would have to teach the class next Sunday. Given what the Bible said, given what this woman had asked, that week turned into a very trying one for my family and me. How could we continue to live in a world with so much need? We were farmers. We grew plants. And here was Christ telling us to love our neighbors. I looked at my own life and asked myself, "What did Jesus do?" He asked the 5,000, "Are you hungry?"—and then he fed them all.

The next Sunday, with the words of 1 John 3:17 still rumbling inside him, Aart Van Wingerden stood before the "Rich Christians" class and said, "I have decided to sell my business. This will allow me and my family to respond to whatever opportunity the Lord has for us in a world with so much need."

"I didn't know what this decision would actually mean," recalls Aart. "I just knew it was the right and only thing we could do."

On Tuesday, some forty-eight hours after Aart announced his news to the Sunday school class, a friend came to the Van Wingerden's home and asked Aart, "Have you ever thought about selling your business?"

"Yes, on Sunday," Aart replied. The two talked. The Van Wingerdens prayed. On Tuesday the sale was complete. Within a few months, Aart and Cornelia and ten of their children moved to Indonesia and discovered the seed of an idea that would change their lives forever. They began working on a 250-acre farm where 600 cows were each producing one gallon of milk per day, less than half of what Aart knew was possible. Not being a dairy expert, he put his farmer's cap on. Aart added limestone to the soil. The grass grew, the cows ate, and within thirteen months, milk production had doubled.

Indonesia was no fluke. The growing methods Aart developed over the next three decades allowed the family greenhouse business to grow, this time in the ideal climate of western North Carolina. Along the way he and Cornelia grew their own family of twelve sons and four daughters. Today, each of the grown sons and sons-in-law owns his own greenhouse business. "I wanted my children to be in competition with me," says Aart. With his wish, the father fueled a dream. Each of the children and their father have invested a portion of their respective business profits into a nonprofit organization called, appropriately, Double Harvest.

Since its founding in 1970, the Van Wingerdens have multiplied food production in Indonesia, Honduras, Haiti, Kenya, Ethiopia, and Zaire.

"The concept of the double harvest," says eldest son Len, "is that people in underdeveloped countries can do better than mere subsistence farming. In the hands of local farmers, the organic, high-tech agricultural methods my father's developed have allowed people to raise more than they need. They can sell the excess and use the profits to support medical clinics and schools they never dreamed of having. In Ethiopia, for instance, resident farmers working with Double Harvest are producing eight to ten times more crops than when they started out, enough to support a local orphanage eighty-five children call home."

Almost every week I meet people who tell me they think their best years are behind them. They're patients and colleagues, friends and acquaintances who say, "I'd *like* to do something different with my life. I just don't know how to take the first step. I don't know where to start."

I listen, I empathize where I can, and then I introduce them to Aart Van Wingerden. I tell them the story of a thirty-five-year-old immigrant forced to feed twelve mouths on six dollars, of a forty-seven-year-old business-man who sold everything out of love and obedience to Jesus. This is the same Aart Van Wingerden, I tell them, who has been living with lung cancer for three years, who still gets up at 6:30 A.M., and who still works each day but Sunday, perfecting growing methods so that food can grow and people can live.

In this down-to-earth man, I see a living lesson of faith that says, "I will listen to my heart. I will step out and trust God. I will take Him at His Word, because I know He loves me and because there's a hunger inside that only He can fill."

I believe you may have more in common with Aart Van Wingerden than you realize, especially if you feel you're at a turning point. Aart's life-changing decision was built on four distinct realizations. Each realization reveals a biblical principle for facing and making important choices in life. Seen as a whole, these principles reveal the loving character of God at work in each step of Aart's decision-making journey and yours.

1. **The Step of Honest Humility: "I don't know the answer."** When the woman in Aart's Sunday school class asked how to put the words of 1 John 3:17 into practice, the teacher was honest. He didn't give her a pat response. He didn't try to pretend he knew more than he did. Instead he said to the woman, and to the class, "I don't know the answer."

   Long journeys and big decisions start with the

words "I don't know." You and I are just like Aart. When confronted with God's truth, we feel inadequate. The truth is, in our limited human understanding we are inadequate. If we can admit this to ourselves and to God, the words "I don't know" can free us rather than panic or defeat us. Instead of turning inward and relying on ourselves for answers, we can turn to God and rely on Him for the understanding, direction, and strength to move ahead.

Aart Van Wingerden knew this and so can you: By admitting you don't know the answer, you can experience the blessing of humility.

Through Aart's humble admission, God turned not knowing into a blessing that touched his entire family and thousands of needy people around the world. The tremendous, continual bounty of Double Harvest is proof of God's command and promise: "Clothe yourselves with humility toward one another, because, 'God opposes the proud / but gives grace to the humble'" (1 Peter 5:5 NIV).

As you look at the rest of your life, how inadequate, how humble do you feel right now?

By humbly admitting, "I don't know the answer," Aart took a second decisive step . . .

2. **The Step of Joyful Obedience: "I will do what God says."** Once Aart admitted he didn't have all the answers, he opened the door to receiving new understanding, opportunity, and direction for himself and his family. Therefore, he knew he could not look to himself; he had to look to God. And in 1 John 3:17, Aart heard God speaking to him: "Whoever has this world's goods, and sees his brother in need, and shuts

up his heart from him, how does the love of God abide in him?"

Aart knew God loved him unconditionally, and it was out of that love that Aart said, "I will obey, I will do what God says." The question of what to do with the rest of your life, facing you now or waiting somewhere down the road, can be filled with anxiety and unknowing. When you come to that turning point, how can feelings of inadequacy allow you to trust God? As Art Van Wingerden discovered, humbleness leads us to the answer:

By knowing that you're loved by a God whose heart and whose Word are love, you can know the joy of obedience.

Taking God at His Word, as Aart and his family did, is not easy. Often, it can be risky, scary, and painful. As Aart found out, you may not know where you're headed. You can know, however, that "He who has begun a good work in you will complete it until the day of Jesus Christ" (Phil. 1:6).

When you think of how God may be humbling you in the big decisions that will shape the rest of your life, how might He be calling you to obedience?

By obeying God, by saying to Him, "My life belongs to You," Aart risked losing himself. Which is exactly what happened . . .

3. **The Step of True Identity: "I know who God made me to be."** When he went to Indonesia, Aart realized that obeying God meant belonging to God. With security, familiarity, and friends removed, he found his true

identity in the gifts God had been developing in him for years. "I realized I do one thing very well," he said. "I'm a farmer."

As you trust your life in humble obedience to the One who knows you and loves you, you can't help but step into true identity.

What's at the heart of *your* true identity today?

If you're willing to trust the very heart of who you are to God, the rest of your life will take care of itself . . .

4. **The Step of Destiny: "Ultimately, my life belongs to God."** Twenty-six years after he had given everything he owned to God, including his future, his family, and his career, Aart Van Wingerden claimed to be one of the richest men alive:

"My life really doesn't belong to me. After the Lord saved me, He bought me—my time, ability, and all my possessions. Whatever I've been given in life does not belong to me. I'm just a steward who's been commanded to share what I have with those who have not. And one day, the Lord will hold me accountable for what He has given me to take care of."

When your humility leads to obedience, and your obedience blossoms into your true identity, you'll be free to ask the question knowing that God has already invested Himself in your destiny.

If you make the courageous choice, as Aart Van Wingerden did—to live your life for the Lord—you may look back on your life and never be totally sure of the difference you made in the world. Don't be surprised, however, if God treats you to the answer, just as he did for a man named Bob Dennis. If you wonder about the meaning of humility, obedience, identity, and destiny in a person's life, this story is for you.

On the morning of May 6, 1945, Bob was seated at the throttle of a B-17 bomber idling on the tarmac of Framlingham, England, sixty miles north of London, on the shore of the English Channel. His plane shared the runway with twenty-three other B-17s and a handful of P-51 escorts. As a twenty-three-year-old first lieutenant, he had every reason to feel nervous. Armistice Day was set for May 8. This would be his first and only mission of the war.

As the plane raced down the runway and lifted off, Bob knew what awaited him and the other members of the 390th Bomber Group one hundred miles to the east. Their destination that morning was the town of Utrecht in the Netherlands. It would not be a pretty sight.

The Germans' decisive victory at the Battle of Dunkirk had brought the Netherlands to its knees. By the spring of 1945, the war in Europe had run its brutal course: thousands of Americans had been killed and wounded. For the Germans, who buried a generation of their own, the cost of war had been just as bitter. For the Netherlands, the end couldn't come soon enough. The Germans had ransacked the tiny, defenseless nation. What little army the country had lay bleeding. To feed its armies, the Germans had eaten virtually the nation's entire food supply. Whole fields of potatoes and rutabagas had been dug up and devoured.

The only things the Dutch had left to eat were sugar beets and tulip bulbs.

News of the starving nation had reached the Red Cross. Realizing their fight was almost over, the Germans agreed to let the Netherlands live once more. They allowed U.S. bombers to drop bundles of rations into fields for the thousands of civilians who had nothing to eat. While the planes flew over, the Germans agreed not to fire on the "Flying Grocery."

Bob Dennis didn't know if the Germans would keep their word. That morning, however, he had no choice but to fly. Forty-five minutes after leaving England's shore, he looked out his cockpit window and saw the final navigational landmark to guide his squadron to their target. There it was, stretched out on the ground, clear and unmistakable. The Dutch had made a giant arrow made entirely out of yellow tulips. This wonderful, brilliant assurance stitched into lonesome green fields pointed to large white Xs made of sheets, where dozens of bundles of food were supposed to land.

Because they came with no parachutes, the payloads would hit hard. So Bob gradually brought his B-17 down from a height of 7,000 feet to 5,000, then 3,000, down to 2,000, down to 1,000, until finally, at 200 feet, the bay doors swung open. Nestled in racks reserved for 8,000 pounds of bombs were containers filled with flour, butter, honey, peanut butter, chocolate, cheese, crackers, and white bread.

The payload dropped.

The planes roared.

The Germans never fired.

As the B-17 climbed out of the drop zone, Bob Dennis

glanced out the left side of the plane. On the ground, spelled out in yellow tulips, were the words "THANKS YANKS."

Bob Dennis was flying too fast that morning to see the men and women run through the fields to their long-awaited feast. He never saw the waving hands or the tears from people below. An hour later, he was back on the ground in England. His life, like the lives of thousands of unseen survivors that morning, would go on. Over the next twenty-seven years, he rose through the Air Force ranks and flew in Korea and Vietnam. In 1972 he retired from the military as a lieutenant colonel.

But other missions lay ahead. When he wasn't tending to his small farm in Cowiche, Washington, Bob gave up evenings at home, restful weekends, and hours on the phone as an elder and deacon at First Presbyterian Church in nearby Yakima. He helped Vietnamese refugees find jobs and safe, new places to live. In June of 1991, he helped a group of local residents build a small two-bedroom home through Habitat for Humanity.

Late one day, before leaving the work site, Bob found himself talking to the project director. "We were almost done with the house," he recalls. "We finished chatting about materials and started talking about our lives. The director looked to be in his early sixties. Since I was only sixty-nine, I figured we would have something in common! I told him I had been a pilot in World War II, that I'd flown one mission. He wanted to know where.

"It was a food drop to help the starving people of the Netherlands. We were called the 'Flying Grocery.'"

The project director, John Van Belle, was silent for a moment. Then he looked at Bob and said, "I know all about that. You see, I was there that day in Rotterdam. I was thirteen years old the morning the U.S. planes flew over. My family had gone without food for days. I was starving. My friends were starving. My father hadn't eaten in several weeks. He was so weak, we expected him to die within days. And then the planes came. He survived. And so did I."

What took place between these two men might be called coincidence, but I believe their rendezvous was a gift of Providence. For the next few minutes, Bob Dennis and John Van Belle stood in the doorway and realized the fullest meaning of a long-ago morning in May. With their eyes still wet, they relived the day when one man's food run had rescued another man's life.

Forty-five years after seeing the ground race beneath his plane's wings, Bob Dennis thought back to an empty field and the sight of yellow tulips. He pictured a starving father, a waiting son, and an anxious pilot somewhere overhead. Then he looked into John Van Belle's eyes. And he knew his mission had been accomplished.

Before you turn the page . . .

If you're presently facing or even considering the possibility of a major life-shaping decision involving a relationship, a job, a possible move, or another important issue, take the next ten minutes to ask yourself the question Jerry and Dee Miller asked themselves: "Can I trust the person(s) making the invitation to be a godly individual with my best interest in mind?" If so, then ask, "Why shouldn't I say yes?"

Ask yourself the question Dean Miller asked himself: "Even though my circumstances may change, what are the God-given gifts I can take with me and use in His service the rest of my life?"

Somewhere, either in the friends you've come to know, the books you've read, or films you've viewed, there's a person like Aart Van Wingerden who, by acting out of humility and obedience, has discovered his or her true identity and destiny in God. How is this individual a model for you as you ask the question, "What will I do with the rest of my life?"

---

† Lydia Brontë, Ph.D. *The Longevity Factor* (New York: HarperCollins Publishers, 1994).

CHAPTER SEVEN

The First Big Step from *Dreaming* to *Doing*

I want you to come with me to the Nanaimo River in Nanaimo, British Columbia, in Canada. On both sides there are steep, forested cliffs that rise almost straight up to the sky. It's to the top of those cliffs that I want us to go. Connecting the two sides is the highest bridge licensed for bungee jumping in North America. You are 142 feet above the river. Step out onto the bridge and walk to the center. There are some people waiting for you with cords. And smiles.

You knew this moment would come. You planned for it, paid for it. You *chose* to do it. You've even told your friends about it. A few are even standing down below on the shores of the Nanaimo River. No need to look down. They're so small you wouldn't recognize them anyway.

Bob, the bungee guide, gives you a big smile and welcomes you to your moment of truth. Now you start to feel it. Your chest is pumping. Your skin is sweating. And now your hands feel cold. You look past Bob and see the bridge railing that's no higher than your waist. There's the bungee cord, wrapped, knotted, and tied to the railing. It looks narrow. It looks thin. If it's so strong, you wonder, why do they need so many ropes braided together?

"Why am I doing this?" you ask yourself. "I don't want to do this." At one time you thought it all through. You still want to go through with it. More like get it over with.

Now Bob attaches the bungee cord to your feet. He wraps your ankles together with a towel. Then he tightens the grip with Velcro straps until you can only teeter on the edge of the bridge.

Everything is ready.

The railing is clear.

The toes of your jogging shoes wiggle out over the edge of the bridge deck.

Bob stands back.

No one's going to force you.

There's nothing holding you back.

Now, you're free to jump . . .

Have you ever stood on the edge of life ready to take the plunge toward a decision you knew was so risky, yet so right? Are you standing there right now? Successful "climbers" like Jerry and Dee Miller, folks in transition like Dean and Carol Miller, people like Bob Dennis who have found a growing joy in helping others—each "bungee jumped" into the unknown. They didn't take the plunge of moving their home, changing jobs, and earning less money because they wanted a cheap thrill. They jumped at the chance of giving up their own security to give to others because somehow they knew it was right. They sensed what you may already know, that life takes on new meaning, purpose, and direction as you take your eyes off yourself and see what God has gifted you with to give to others.

Here's the frustration that brings us to the turning point in this book, and perhaps a turning point in your life. You may be totally convinced that it's right to live for others and *still* live unhappily the rest of your life, second-guessing yourself, thinking, "I could have . . . I should have . . . I might have . . ." because you never took the plunge.

Do the bungee cords around your ankles suddenly feel a little tighter? I'm not going to force you to jump. I simply want you to see that you have a choice. You can keep standing on the bridge of life, afraid that God won't catch you if you make the leap. Or you can give all that you are to all that you know of God and let the full weight of your decision carry you to do something risky and adventurous with your life.

How do you do that? How do you move from *dreaming* to *doing*? I believe a person like Aart Van Wingerden has already given us the answer. In chapter 6, his four-step decision-making process of "letting go and letting God" is a revealing, accurate picture of what it means to take the leap:

For Aart Van Wingerden, as well as for you and me, the real turning point in our lives will take place when we're willing to admit, "I don't know what lies ahead."

- *By admitting "I don't know the answer"* we are blessed with a spirit of **destiny**.

- In humility, *by doing what the Bible says* we are driven by a life of **obedience**.

112

- Through obedience, *by focusing on our God-given talent* we are assured of our true **identity**.

- Because of identity, *by realizing we're not really owners but stewards* we are reminded of our ultimate **destiny**.

This wonderful sequence of how God can take us from confusion to blessing is the story of how Aart Van Wingerden has lived a life of distinction. Are you content to merely know this truth? Or would you like to experience God's meaning, purpose, and direction for yourself for the *rest of your life?*

The secret is having the courage to take the first and often most difficult step. The secret is *to act*. In my lifetime I can think of two people who did just this, who found themselves in the exact same spot that Aart Van Wingerden, as well as you and I, had been. These two individuals could not be more different from each other, one a well-to-do homemaker in southern California, and the other a struggling Mexican pastor from south Texas. Yet, as both were faced with the fact that death could come at any moment, both in their own way admitted, "Lord, I don't know the answer."

In the face of certain tragedy, their personal, unlikely triumphs reveal that the courage to live comes naturally from God because *the rest of our lives really belong to Him!* As you read their stories, Aart Van Wingerden's discoveries will take on a new meaning, as you see how

- your humility is the human face of His power,

- your obedience is the human face of His companionship,

- your identity as steward is the human face of His abundance, and
- your destiny is the human face of His love.

Before I can tell their stories, I must first share with you my own story of the first and most risky step—I almost didn't take.

My "bungee jump" came in the summer of 1985. It did not happen on a bridge in Nanaimo, British Columbia, staring 142 feet down at sharp rocks and nervous water. It was much scarier than that.

For the previous eighteen years, I had enjoyed an exciting, sometimes whirlwind, yet mostly rewarding career. Relying on my own determination, wisdom, and appetite to set goals and then to reach them, I had successfully navigated life's white water. After twenty-six years of medicine, I had reached a wide, serene bend in the river. I could float the rest of my days, enjoy the sunshine, and cast my cares to a lazy current. I had fought my way through every rapid in my path. At fifty-two years old, I was tired, fulfilled, and happy. I was ready to coast.

But something happened. One workday morning, while reading the morning paper, I was channel surfing with the remote control. Somewhere between a cooking show and a car commercial, I caught the face of a man. I flicked the channel to take a second look. It was him. How uncanny. He looked so much like his famous father, just younger. His name in the on-screen graphic confirmed it. The sound was on "mute," so I turned up the volume. The face of Franklin Graham began to talk to me. About pockets of unseen poverty in the world. About naked, desperate children and numbed parents who died from intestinal parasites, malaria, and malnutrition every day because they had never seen a physician.

That morning, in my spacious Ventura home, I woke up to hot coffee and warm California sun, while the idea of floating comfortably into retirement continued to make me more and more uncomfortable. I sat up in bed and heard the beat of my own heart. The man on the television, a man I had never met, who knew my profession, was asking me to bungee jump.

I knew what it would mean to take the plunge: giving up at least six weeks from my private practice—a sizable chunk of income and the comfortable routine I was used to—and paying my own way to treat sick patients in a third-world setting much different from my own.

My decision to go translated into our family of five making the same commitment. The surprise came when I found they didn't need me in a bush hospital in Africa. "We need *'real doctors,'* not brain surgeons," was the word from Franklin Graham's staff. "Maybe we can use you as a visiting professor in a Presbyterian mission hospital in South Korea."

All I knew about Korea was that I had been fortunate in not having to go fight there during the "Korean Conflict." Arriving there, we found everything different from what we were accustomed to.

When we arrived back home in Ventura, our friends asked the same question: "What was it like?" I couldn't find words to capture the sights, smells, and emotions I had experienced. All I had were a few indelible images, moving pictures, forever frozen in time.

Some of the South Korean Christians woke up at four o'clock in the morning to worship and pray before their workday began, the sound of voices singing, "Ho-rey, Ho-rey, Hoooo-rey" (Holy, Holy, Holy) drifting up through open windows while the sky was still black.

Eating raw fish that had been dried in the sun, soup with bits of sea creatures and things unidentifiable floating in it, and more steamed rice than I ever thought existed was different. The heat and high humidity, interrupted by violent thunderstorms with rain so heavy you could hardly see was different. On Tuesdays at noon, it was the wail of air-raid sirens and low-flying fighter aircraft as a reminder of the ever-present danger of renewed fighting with the North. Many things required some adjustment for our family from California.

But the thing that overwhelmed us was the polite hospitality of the people—the gracious way in which they received us into their culture, giving us gifts at every opportunity. Then, there was the deep commitment of the Korean Christian people; a commitment that made us realize that even though we were the missionaries, we were the ones who were being ministered to.

We were drawn to Dr. David Seel, the missionary surgeon who also served as medical director of the hospital. Keeping up with him was a challenge, as he walked briskly from administrative offices to patient wards to outpatient clinics and then stood for hours in the operating room before seeming to start the process all over again. His wife, Mary, who had served at her husband's side for twenty-six years, would smile and say, "These are my people. I love each one of them. David and I thank God every day for blessing us with this opportunity of serving Him in helping those who otherwise would not have help."

And then, the most piercing image of all. The quiet face

of a middle-aged man named Mr. Lee. He worked in the hospital laundry. Several years earlier, his only son had been killed by a speeding truck as he crossed the street outside the hospital. Mr. Lee didn't spend the insurance money from the trucking company on himself; he chose to use it to build a beautiful small chapel building on the wooded hillside nearby. As construction neared completion, money ran out. Mr. Lee came to Dr. Seel one night with a proposal. "I have decided to sell one of my eyes to someone who is losing his vision. I have nothing else to give that might raise the money necessary to provide for the completion of the chapel's construction. It is more important that people have a place to worship than that I be able to see."

The thought hit me: suppose I had never gone to South Korea? Suppose I had never decided to call a "time-out" on ninety-hour work-weeks that were leaving me breathless and fatigued. Suppose I had never decided to give up the income, leave my upper-middle-class cocoon in suburbia, and, with my family, step into a foreign culture called "Jesu Pyongwon" (Jesus Hospital). Had I not taken this plunge, I wouldn't be able to appreciate the story of one woman's life whose turning point showed me what it meant to really start living.

Storybook. In a word, that was Diane Bringgold's life. In the fall of 1975 she and her husband, Bruce, lived in a nice hillside home in Ventura, California. They were our next-door neighbors. Our children played together in the vacant lot between our two houses.

Bruce was a young, ambitious attorney. Following graduation from law school, he began as an attorney in the D.A.'s office. Two years later he was a partner in a

Ventura law firm. Diane worked as an institutional parole agent for the Youth Authority at the Ventura School for girls until the birth of her first child, when she "retired" to focus on being a wife and mother. The Bringgolds had arrived in Ventura with all their earthly possessions loaded inside their 1959 Volkswagen. Within a few years, however, their real worth increased dramatically in three increments:

First, there was Scott. The spittin' image of his father. Loved to hunt with Dad. Loved sports. Played sports. Breathed sports. Adored as a first child, cherished as a son.

Then, three years later, a daughter, Mary. Very serious. Liked to turn Mother's kitchen into a cooking club. Five or six third graders messing up Mom's kitchen. And making Mom feel included in their adventure.

And three years later, a second daughter, Laura. Brunette. Affectionate. Loved her brother and sister. Shared a bedroom with them until another room was added to their home five months before the accident. Yes, the accident.

It happened on a Monday. Diane, Bruce, Scott, Mary, and Laura were seated snugly inside a Cessna 210 with friends Jim and Virginia Dixon. They had just spent a weekend with close friends, the LeFevres, at their vacation home in Dunsmuir, near Mt. Shasta in northern California. They had planned to leave Sunday. On Saturday it snowed. By Monday afternoon, the low overcast was clearing as they took off. But as quickly as they had seemed to clear, the low-lying clouds moved in again. As a worried Bruce tried to make his flight path follow the outline of Highway 5, a thousand feet below, Diane grew more quiet, more tense.

Suddenly they had no visibility. Then, the moment that

changed her life. A moment without any warning of what the next twenty years would bring. A moment only Diane, herself, could describe:

> "Oh my God, Bruce, the trees!"
>
> I screamed. Bruce, at the controls, saw them too. Instantly, he reacted, banking the plane sharply left, but not in time to avoid the onrushing mountainside.
>
> I remember the crash landing did not seem as rough as I expected. Then . . . it was all over . . . the end . . . the end of everything . . . nothing . . .
>
> I don't know how long I was unconscious, but probably no more than a few moments. Suddenly, I was aware of the flames bursting out from below the instrument panel. I still had my seat belt on, but I had slid down in my seat. Bruce was leaning on top of me. He wasn't moving. There was no sound at all in the plane except the crackling of the flames. They were searing my legs, my hands, my face. Instinctively I had thrown my hands over my eyes. Somehow, wriggling and squirming, I got my seat belt unfastened and pushed Bruce off me. He still did not move.
>
> I slid out the open door and crawled away from the plane seconds before the gas tanks exploded.

The Cessna had smashed into Black Butte Mountain. The crash and aftermath. Cold air and flames. The distant sounds of cars passing by on Highway 5. The excruciating pain in Diane's face, hands, and legs. Eventually a needle with one shot of morphine administered by a physician who had made his way in the dark to the crash scene. And then, pain that morphine couldn't take away. Bruce, Scott, Mary, and Laura had all been killed.

This was not her only grief. Thirty percent of her body

had been burned. For the next sixty days, Diane remained wrapped in multiple layers of bandages. Her right hand was so badly burned the doctor was not sure he could save it. The first skin grafts came twenty-four hours after the crash. Five weeks in intensive care, unable to feed herself or wipe the part of her nose that had not been burned away, Diane Bringgold began to mark the passages of a new life:

Leaving the hospital six weeks after she had entered, to live in a local Holiday Inn.

Feeling the uncomfortable pressure of special elastic garments and a face mask designed to help the grafted skin to heal smoothly.

Waking up at four o'clock in the morning to wash and rinse her one set of pressure garments and then climbing back into bed to sleep in comfort while they dried.

Taking twenty minutes to pull up her stockings, one inch at a time with her left hand because she could not yet use her badly burned right hand.

Coming back home. Revisiting each of her children's bedrooms, and then remembering what her own bed used to feel like.

Sylvia and I had invited Diane and Bruce to dinner on the Sunday before the crash on Black Butte Mountain. We talked about flying. We talked about our children. We reminisced about our time together at Mt. Shasta for the Fourth of July holidays the previous summer. Now, on Diane's first night back home, we invited her for dinner.

"Diane, the Benefactors Ball to benefit the hospital is next Saturday night. Would you like to come with Sylvia and me?" Before the words were halfway out of my mouth, I wondered what had prompted me to ask the question, and I wondered what her response would be. "That would be great," she said with a smile. "It will be an opportunity to see all of *our* friends."

Diane went with us to the charity ball. She wore an elastic body jacket under her gown and a smile on her face. I know there must have been very difficult times for her in the months and years that followed, but never did we hear her complain. It was as if God had blessed her in her time of grief and had surrounded her with a love so powerful that, with His help, she could handle anything. Many people didn't know what to say to Diane, but she always had the kindness and the good grace to make them feel comfortable. Just being with her was a great inspiration.

But perhaps the most significant event of all came fourteen months after the accident. In February 1977, Ruth Borchert, an aunt of Bruce's, invited Diane to share her story with a small group at St. Olaf's Lutheran Church in Garden Grove. "Before the accident I was terrified of making a fool of myself," she reflected. Now, she merely felt panicked. Diane walked into her study and prayed that the Lord would give her direction. He did, through words He had spoken years earlier to the twelve disciples when He said, "Do not worry about what to say or how to say it. At that time you will be given what to say, for it will not be you speaking, but the Spirit of your Father speaking through you" (Matt. 10:19–20 NIV).

The irony of these words is that God was preparing Diane to share the very words He had said to her in the frightening, cold moments of the plane crash. In her first public talk, Diane took the people of St. Olaf's back to the mountainside. She probably did not realize that what she was about to share that afternoon would be a gift to anyone else who has ever felt inadequate about what to do when your life is at a turning point.

Aware that her own husband and three children were now dead, Diane said:

> I crawled away from the flames and behind a large rock to die. There I placed the back of my hands on the snow-covered rock to ease the pain. I wished it were colder so I could freeze to death quickly.
>
> Suddenly something caused me to look up. About eight or ten feet away, I saw a white-robed figure. The figure was radiant, but the radiance did not dispel the fog. It seemed to be a man, though I couldn't distinguish His features clearly. Somehow I knew it was the Lord.
>
> "Diane." His voice was warm but full of authority. "It is not up to you to decide whether to live or die. That decision is Mine alone to make."
>
> I don't know why, but somehow I was not surprised that He was there with me, that He was speaking to me. I wanted Him to know that I really couldn't go on living. "Lord, that's easy for you to say, but I can't face being widowed, being childless, and being badly burned. Two out of three maybe, but not all three." I wasn't trying to bargain with Him. I did not expect Him to restore my husband or my children or to heal me, although He could have. I just wanted Him to know it was the combination of circumstances that had overwhelmed me.
>
> He remained silent, as if He were waiting for me to continue. "Lord," I said, "if you want me to live, I will give you my life. I will give you my problems. You will have to cope with the pain, the loneliness, and with the grief. I can't." Still He did not speak, but such love flowed from Him that I knew He would care for me—that He would handle the grief, the pain, the loneliness. I knew that I was in His care and that

everything would be all right. . . . As suddenly as He had appeared, the Lord was no longer there. I don't know how long He had been with me there on the mountain—a few minutes or a few seconds. Time was unimportant.[†]

You and I may never meet the Lord in such a personal, dramatic way. Yet, I believe you and I share something very basic with Diane Bringgold. If you sit with her on the side of that mountain for a few minutes and listen to her response to the Lord, I think her words can speak directly to how you may choose to live your life differently in the coming weeks and months.

If you're seriously asking yourself, "What will I do with the rest of my life?" because you believe your reason for being here on earth has more to do with others and less with self, you'll likely answer the question in one of two ways. The first is to embark on what I like to call "a life of change." Feeling unfulfilled and unsatisfied with themselves, those who answer this way take on an ambitious overhaul of their values and lifestyle. With well-intentioned motives, they set out to change how they spend their time, energy, and money. These are virtuous choices. They represent a sincere desire to think less of getting and think more of giving.

Despite the fact I had changed the way I was investing my time, money, and energy; despite a definite change of heart to do less for Mel Cheatham and more for others; one thing hadn't changed. I was still working too hard. I was still tired, still out of breath. Every time I got involved in a short-term mission project there was still "so much more to do." I had "bungee jumped" into a life of service, yet I wondered what had really changed inside me. I knew

God wanted me to live for Him; I just didn't believe He wanted me to continue to run myself ragged in the process. Maybe that's why Diane Bringgold's story had such a powerful impact on me.

Lying helpless on a ground of fire and ice, wondering if her life was damaged beyond repair, Diane showed there is another way to live the rest of your life. Her approach has nothing to do with increased ambition, but with a much different, more authentic, and surprising catalyst for living. It has to do with knowing that we are ultimately powerless to control our own destiny. It has to do with humility. It has to do with being human. It has to do with the fact that once we are stripped of all our creature comforts, our titles, our reputations, we see how helpless we really are—and how much we need God.

A life motivated by pure ambition may produce a changed lifestyle. A life motivated by pure humility, however, can produce a changed heart.

A life driven by ambition may leave you feeling more important and more valuable because of something you did for God. A life rooted in humility, however, can make you feel grateful and honored to be part of something He's already doing in your life and in others', something that's greater than any achievement you or I could muster.

It was the realization that premature death might be my reward for riding the runaway train of ambition and success that led me to experience humility. Throughout my career, I had always felt that it was I who was in control. I liked being in control. It felt good. But not good enough to die for. Turning toward a life of giving to others, instead of living for me, meant surrendering control to God. This translated into humility and also to a sense of purpose and fulfillment, free from the fears and the pressures of trying to determine my own destiny.

The time is coming, perhaps it's already come, when you'll be brought to your knees. You probably won't be shivering on the side of a mountain, like Diane Bringgold. Your own humble terrain may be less dramatic but no less urgent: a rocky marriage, a career that seems dried up, a self-image that's so low you may feel Diane had stolen your words when she said, "I just wanted [the Lord] to know it was the combination of circumstances that had overwhelmed me."

Being humble does not mean being defeated. With God, being humble means you are free to really live. When you reach the point of saying, "Only you, God, can help me," then, because He wants you to live, Diane Bringgold's response becomes the freeing voice of humility:

"Lord, if you want me to live, I will give you my life. I will give you my problems. You will have to cope with the pain, with the loneliness, and with the grief. I can't."

As Aart Van Wingerden and others who felt so inadequate have discovered, once we've become humbled, we become obedient out of love to the One who loves us. Suddenly, we see it:

In **our humility** we see *His* greatness.

Out of **our obedience** we find *His* companionship.

Just as Diane did: "Still He did not speak, but such love flowed from Him that I knew He would care for me—that He would handle the grief, the pain, the loneliness. I knew that I was in His care and that everything would be all right."

If you want to know what happens to someone who takes the plunge and trusts God with the rest of her life, look at Diane Bringgold. For ten years after the accident, Diane remained alone. She experienced loneliness, anger, and moments of wanting to give up. But always in her loneliness and anger, in her times of doubt and uncertainty, she turned to God, asking His help, His guidance, and found her prayers answered. This was not a storybook ending, but a long-enduring chapter of being human and remaining humble. Her greatest fear was standing up in front of an audience and telling her story. Yet, over the last twenty years she has stood before hundreds of groups. "Most of us," she tells the audience, "are raised to be self-reliant. As long as we handle things, we don't need His love. Yet, now that you've heard my story, you know that I have no other option than to live the rest of my life for Him."

Today, with her new husband, Don Brown, Diane travels around the United States leading retreats, helping Christians identify and use their spiritual gifts as well as live out their baptismal vows, to proclaim by word and deed the Word of God in Christ.

Diane Bringgold shows me *by her life* what it means to live in humbleness and in obedience to God. She would be the first to tell you that if you allow the Lord to take on loneliness, your questions, your future, choosing to live the rest of your life serving Him and others will not be easy. But it will be real, and true, and right, because as you live your life for Him, you'll become a new person with a new direction.

Diane showed me what it meant to take first steps of humility and obedience. It was another person working in the baking dust of war-torn Honduras who, like Diane, showed me that humbleness and obedience are central in knowing our true identity in God and in living a life that counts.

In October 1987, I found myself on a 110-seat plane from Miami bound for Tegucigalpa, Honduras, in Central America. As the plane descended from the clouds, I could see the lush green hills and mountains below. This land was home to a two-year-old civil war, and I was one of two physicians whom Franklin Graham had asked to accompany him on a preliminary relief trip for Samaritan's Purse and World Medical Mission. We were met by soldiers from the Contra Guerilla Army who transported us to a remote place called Big Camp. This was the military outpost where Contra casualties were brought after their battlefield wounds were healed. There were many of these young people, men and women, whose average age I reckoned to be about nineteen. Some had lost eyes, others limbs. Some were permanently paralyzed.

Around their necks, these young soldiers wore crosses hammered out of M16 shell casings. In one of the buildings there were dozens of wooden coffins, constructed on the spot and waiting for future casualties. "The coffin I build now as my wounds heal may become my permanent resting place later, after I go back to the fighting," one of the young men said to me.

At the frontline hospital, I walked down row after row of bandaged and bleeding men and women. Some had no arms or legs. Others stared up from hollow eyes, unaware that infection or malnourishment would soon claim them. But this horror was just a prelude to what would happen moments later.

Our group was led to the quarters of Dr. Henry, a physician who was also the commandant of the Contra

Guerilla Army unit. It was a small room, no more than eight feet by ten feet. There was a single bunk bed and a small table and chair. He invited us to hold his machine guns. We obliged. As Dr. Henry stood there telling us about the great needs for medical assistance, he casually tossed a live hand grenade up and down. "If the metal pin in this thing falls out," he said confidently, "we've got three seconds before it explodes." I wasn't sure whether Dr. Henry just had great hand-eye coordination or if he had a death wish. Without the protocol, or courage, I wasn't the one to ask him to stop.

"Why don't you put the grenade down so I can take a picture of it?" I said. I laid the machine gun I was holding down next to the grenade, which Dr. Henry had placed on his bunk. As I focused my camera, a man named Brother Reuben grabbed my arm and said, "Wait a minute, Doc." Positioning his big, black Bible between the grenade and the gun, he said, "Now take the picture. If there's an answer to this war, it's the gospel of Jesus Christ."

I looked at this guy and asked myself, *How could one man's faith make any difference?* When he told me his story the following day, I was shocked by what I heard—shocked and a little embarrassed that I had ever doubted the impact one person could make on his world.

Brother Reuben's journey began in a chapel service of a small Bible school he was attending in San Antonio, Texas. That morning, he heard about cities in the world that had no missionaries. "This pricked my heart," he said. "Instead of returning to classes, I stayed and prayed, 'Lord, if there's a place in the world where others can't go or won't go, I'll go.' Little did I know what my prayer would mean."

As the Cuban refugee crisis was beginning to build, a

woman in his Dallas church prayed, "Get Brother Reuben into Cuba, or get the Cubans out." Within a few weeks, he got a phone call asking if he would be able to preach to Cuban refugees who were to be housed at Ft. Smith, Arkansas. "For the next year and a half, I was given the opportunity to preach the gospel and set up Bible studies for 17,000 refugees," he recalls. It was all a preparation for things to come.

Things he couldn't see until he traveled to Nicaragua and came face-to-face with the broken spirits and barren shells of men, women, and children—entire families who were dying from civil strife.

Lord, if there's a place in the world where others can't go or won't go, I'll go.

Then came another opportunity that had God's fingerprints all over it. Bill Murray, a committed Christian and son of atheist Madalyn Murray O'Hair, met Brother Reuben and agreed to fund a preaching mission to Honduras. There Brother Reuben saw the horror of teenage boys without limbs, without hope, some blind, others totally scarred for life. "When I looked at them," he said, "I thought about my own children."

Six months later, another piece of the puzzle, another divine surprise. Brother Reuben met a worker from the Christian Broadcasting Network who told him that Pat Robertson had been praying for one person to minister to the soldiers in Honduras. Reuben could not tell the journalist if he was that man, but he gave him his name.

Lord, if there's a place in the world where others can't go or won't go, I'll go.

"The next day I got a call from a human rights resistance group asking if I would be interested in evangelizing all

20,000 in the Nicaraguan military." The official told Brother Reuben, "I've been given authority to invite you to preach and do whatever you feel is necessary to bring the gospel and Christian ethics to our men, because they need to know what it means to live right." The place where no one else wanted to go, the place where Brother Reuben found himself in February 1986, was a network of treacherous mountain roads, sprinkled with land mines, that took him deep into Honduras to military bases. The first day, he preached to several thousand men and hundreds raised their hands as a sign of their decision to accept Jesus Christ as their Savior and Lord.

During that first week, one of the young soldiers came up to Brother Reuben. He looked to be about twenty. He wore tired, rumpled fatigues. The brightest thing about him was his eager smile. He said to Brother Reuben, "I like to sing and I want to help you lead the music." However, the young man didn't know any of the chords. Brother Reuben might have forgotten the youth except for one thing.

"What's your name?" Brother Reuben asked.

"My name is Hitler," said the young man.

"You mean like the German Nazi?"

"Yes, it was given to me as my code name."

Brother Reuben and Hitler spent the next several weeks together traveling to various sites where soldiers heard a message of forgiveness and love that had nothing to do with the war they were fighting and everything to do with their lives. Brother Reuben was never quite sure what Hitler believed or where he was going when he disappeared into the countryside. Three months went by and Brother Reuben was preaching to 300 men one day. In the very back row, he could see the tiny shape of a person calling out to him. The figure grew larger as he moved toward the preacher. Brother Reuben remembered the smile. It was Hitler.

Hitler and Brother Reuben embraced. This time Hitler not only knew the songs by heart, he had brought his own musicians. With the audience of 300 still seated, Brother Reuben turned to the men and said, "Today, Hitler is going to lead us in our songs." But Hitler started shaking his head. "No, no, no," he whispered to Brother Reuben who seemed confused—until Hitler explained.

"The reason I'm saying no is because I'm no longer 'Hitler.' My name is now Lazarus, because I've been resurrected. Once I was dead. But thanks to Jesus Christ I'm now alive."

Lord, if there's a place in the world where others can't go or won't go, I'll go.

It's fair to say that because Brother Reuben found his place in the world, the special place where no one else would go, a young man named Hitler found the Savior named Jesus. The new Lazarus learned the Bible like he had learned songs, with eagerness and devotion. Under Brother Reuben's guidance over the next several months, Lazarus directed 119 chaplains. Today, he is a pastor in Nicaragua.

In Honduras today there are thousands of people who, like the man who was once called Hitler, could answer to the name Lazarus because of one man named Brother Reuben. Think of it: one humble student sitting in a chapel service saying, "Yes, Lord, I'll go wherever You want. I'll sacrifice anything, even if it would take me from my wife and children, because my life belongs to You." What happened to Brother Reuben? How was he able to go from the willing desire to serve to an opportunity of profound influence? What enabled him, prepared him, and empowered him to experience what we all long for, and that's before our life is done, to fulfill the deepest longings of our heart?

I believe the answer begins on the shale-covered side of Black Butte Mountain and comes to rest in the sun-drenched flatlands of Honduras. Diane Bringgold and Brother Reuben are living "the rest of their lives" because they took small, practical steps toward God when they seemed unable and unsure of what they were doing. When Aart Van Wingerden took those same steps of humble obedience, God honored his decision by multiplying his opportunities to share his talents with others. God did the same thing for Brother Reuben. Once he knew his life was not his own, Brother Reuben found his true identity. Discovering where he was supposed to be wasn't his responsibility anymore. Like his identity, his destiny was now in Someone else's hands. In fact there is a very logical relationship between the two.

The process of discovering your true identity in God puts you on a pathway of service that leads to a destiny reserved only for you.

Discovering what to do and how to live the rest of your life *is* a process. Making the Big Decision, whether it's entering marriage, starting a family, or changing careers, may feel like bungee jumping off a 142-foot bridge. Commitment always looks like a huge, terrifying leap *before* you make it! Most of life's momentous turning points actually take place through a series of small, important choices:

- Reading a book that sparks an option you never thought about

- Keeping a prior lunch date with a friend whose life is at a crossroads

- Making the time for your child and discovering he has something to tell you

- Creating a place for the person you'll meet, the Scripture you'll read, the quiet you'll enjoy, and discovering that in each of these common, everyday moments God has something to reveal about where He wants to lead you

Deciding what to do with the rest of your life could bring a major-league change in your zip code, your appointment calendar, and your bank account. If you start to feel paralyzed, remember Diane Bringgold and Brother Reuben and the changes they went through. When I see these two people, I see what true faithfulness looks like when we freely admit to God, "I don't know what lies ahead." When saying those words, we feel like we're seconds away from a first bungee jump; we're forced to depend on God.

If God could lead Diane Bringgold off the side of a mountain and sustain her through months of painful skin grafting, do you think He is able and willing to come near you and give your life new direction and meaning in the days ahead?

If God could shape the destiny of Brother Reuben—who knew nothing more than that God might send him some place no one else wanted to go—do you think God is able to guide you through a series of small, yet important steps to a place He's reserved just for you?

And if God can work in the life of an ambitious neuro-surgeon and change his heart of ambition into one of obedience, I know he is able and willing to do great things in your life. If he changed the heart of Hitler, will He not change you?

Before you turn the page . . .

Take a closer look at the major ideas, possible opportunities, and looming decisions you've been thinking about as you've read this chapter. In chapter 6, you identified your God-given gifts and looked at the question, *"Why shouldn't I say yes* to an opportunity put before me by a trusted, godly individual?" You also considered some specific individuals who made similar choices for themselves out of humble obedience.

Now, think again: What is the Big Decision facing you? Write it out on a piece of paper. As you think about your response ask:

- Can you come to God humbly saying, "I don't know the answer"?

- Can you come to God obediently saying, "I'll trust you with this decision"?

Whether it feels like you're making a bungee jump or a small step of faith, your Big Decision marks a possible turning point for the rest of your life, because your new identity rests with a God who knows your destiny and who will guide you to that unique place where no one else can go.

[†] From Diane Bringgold, *Life Instead* (Colorado Springs, CO: Howard Publications, 1984); reproduced with kind permission of the author.

CHAPTER EIGHT

The Freedom to Love Without Expecting Something in Return

The changed lives of Brother Reuben and Diane Bring-gold are truly inspiring. But to anyone who believes it's possible to make his or her life really count for something, their stories also present a potential problem. Think of Reuben or Diane, or a friend, colleague, or peer you've read about or seen in the news. When we see these everyday people move beyond their mundane, comfortable existence to a life of serving others, a silent admiration begins to build inside of us. The script goes kind of like this:

"I really respect what she's doing."

"I can't believe how God has gifted him."

"What they're doing is incredible."

As we admire someone who's involved in the kinds of things we could be about, we begin to look more closely at ourselves and think:

"What am I doing with my life?"

"What would I have to *do* to change my little corner of the world?"

This is the place where a lot of people, including myself, are tempted to get stuck. This is the potential snag that comes from desiring to move from a life of largely serving ourselves to serving others.

Once we realize what's good, what's right, and what's possible to accomplish—once we see someone whose faith and courage inspire us to act—we want to know what to do. "If I just started to *do* things a little differently," we conclude, "if I change the way I live, then I could break through my old patterns, habits, self-image, and fears—all the things that keep me from taking the risk and taking hold of the opportunity before me. But first I need to know what to *do*."

The problem with this kind of thinking is that we've been raised in a how-to culture that has reduced the meaning of life to a cooking recipe. Our lives are so rushed, our time so limited, we want "Instant Life Direction—Just add pat answers, determination, and stir." There's nothing instant about the extraordinary and lasting life changes that have come to people like Brother Reuben and Diane Bringgold and Aart Van Wingerden and Jerry and Dee Miller. The extraordinary changes you'll experience as you give yourself to others are not the result of "doing something" out of guilt, the need to comply, or impulsiveness that acts without thinking.

A life that counts, a life of using your distinctive gifts and your heart for God to touch the hearts of others, is not reached by mastering a set of predictable how-tos; *it's discovered by weighing the needs of others against an opportunity to serve and asking, "What if?"*

A life that counts is not a monument built on self-assurance of what you can do on your own; *it's a living testimony of what God can do through you.*

A life that counts is not a virtuous exercise in good deeds you do because of what you stand to gain; *it's a conscious choice of sacrifice and personal satisfaction that's defined by what you'll most certainly give up along the way.*

If you're willing to take this path of adventuresome faith—not the path of stove-top solutions, but the patient path of dedication and sacrifice—I can assure you of one thing. Your decision to serve others will leave you tired, frustrated, and at times wondering, "Did I really make a difference?" In the next few pages, as you meet some everyday people who asked themselves this very question, the answer will become obvious.

Some people know their calling in life from day one. Some, like Dick Rathman, don't make the discovery until their lives are half over. After graduating from college, Dick spent four years as a chemist, followed by two more as a chemical engineer. "I really enjoyed my work as a chemist but then came to realize that my real satisfaction came from my contact with people." It was this love for people that led Dick to reconsider the question of what he was going to do with the rest of his life. When he was forty-one years old, he took a psychological inventory. "I wanted to find out whether my talents and abilities would lend themselves to some other type of work that was more 'people oriented.'"

The results were startling. "I found out I was interested in persuasive sales more than 99.9 percent of the general population," says Dick. Translation: he was a born salesman. At an age when most career people start thinking ahead to their retirement, Dick's career was just beginning.

THE FREEDOM TO LOVE . . .

Dick's persuasive personality, along with his high technical aptitude, made him a perfect fit for a new career in insurance, handling employee benefits.

Imagine the incredible breakthrough Dick must have felt. For many years you do a job in a semi-satisfied way. Then one day you discover something you always sensed was true but never really knew for sure. You not only identify and affirm two distinct talents—a sincere love for people and a keen knack for numbers—you see them come together in a brand-new line of work! For Dick, the best news of all is that the discovery of his gifts didn't just mean a new job—it opened up a whole new way to live.

> Always, my philosophy about selling is that I don't sell unless I have the best possible product. In that way I maintain my integrity. If I don't believe it, I don't sell it. The reason is I'm not in business to make a quick sale. I'm in it for the long-term relationships I've built with my clients. In my work, it just makes sense. When you're helping someone plan their pension fund and retirement, you have to look toward the future. You have to help folks realize where they are today in relation to what they'll have to live on down the road. A lot of people don't think their lives will end someday. People think they're going to live forever.

They don't. In May 1994, life's road suddenly became a lot shorter for Dick Rathman. At age seventy-four he was told he had colon and liver cancer. The doctors gave him two years to live.

"Suddenly we thought more seriously about life," says Dick's wife, Dorothy. "We no longer looked at life as 'What are we planning to do a year from now?' It was

'What are we going to do today?'" For Dick, himself, the cancer couldn't have come at a worse time.

"When I turned seventy, I had been signing up employee benefit packages with hospitals for forty-one years. I felt like I was just in the prime of my career. I didn't need to retire; I wanted to keep working and keep living!" Dick had one problem. He didn't know whether to agree to a twenty-year extension that would take him to ninety-one years old, or to settle on a mere ten-year extension so he could keep working until he was eighty-one! Today the cancer is in remission. "My doctor has just told me that I am his 'number one' best result among his cancer chemotherapy patients and that I am also 'number one' when it comes to attitude." Dorothy adds, "We know that Dick has done so incredibly well because of so many prayers for him and because of his consistently positive attitude—*and* my good cooking, of course." For Dick Rathman, "the rest of his life," from his mid-thirties on, has been a life of distinction.

This is a man who invests in relationships by buying tickets to the Chicago Symphony, the Chicago Opera, and Chicago Cubs baseball games. When Dick Rathman's friends go to the mailbox, they find an envelope with their name on it. Inside is a handwritten note and a gift of love.

This is the man who, with his wife, established a home for the mentally retarded thirty-eight years ago, a home that now has one hundred patients. He has served on the school board, four years as its president. Raising financial support for those in need has been a lifelong avocation, and Dick Rathman counts 135 charitable organizations with which he has worked. With the stroke of a pen, Dick and Dorothy substantially funded a brain tumor research laboratory during a time of critical need, allowing important work to continue. "Dorothy and I really haven't done that much, but every time we give to others, it seems to come back to bless us ten times over." Dorothy adds, "Helping others is the real secret for not only staying healthy and happy but even to staying alive as you get older."

Dick Rathman is the man who recently went out to the golf course on a Saturday morning and broke a score of one hundred. Some people accomplish the feat with help of a friendly mulligan (or two). Dick played every hole with a five-pound chemotherapy machine strapped to his back.

This is a man who's planning on keeping his customers satisfied into his eighties, even though his doctors gave him only two years to live. This is the man whose ready smile, hearty laugh, and positive attitude seem to cancel out the nausea, fatigue, and depression that others frequently experience during chemotherapy. "The only thing I begrudge in life is having to go to Northwestern University Hospital every week for my treatments—I sure would like to have that time available to do things for other people."

When I look at Dick Rathman, I am sold on the importance, the meaning, and the joy of serving others. For a man who could be preoccupied with dying, Dick is totally consumed with living. Often during the week, he will sit at his desk and spend ten, twenty, even thirty minutes writing. This is time he could be spending on himself. Since learning of his cancer, Dick has regularly given up the chance to go golfing, to take a walk, or read a good book so that he might spend the time writing dozens of poems for friends. On a recent day, my fax machine hummed unexpectedly. Within half a minute, I was holding half a lifetime of wisdom and caring. Though the poem had my name on it, the words are for you and for anyone who wants his or her life to count:

What Will You Do with the Rest of Your Life?

As a salesman I always feel
The income derived from the sale,
But what contributes to my zeal,
A thankful client makes the money pale.

How then can I go on living
If a sale cannot be made?
By concentrating on giving,
But still call a spade a spade.

If ever I feel lonely,
Down-hearted or blue,
I have but one wish only,
To be at one with You.

What if the doctor's statement
Of my two year demise,
Would have no hope of abatement?
This is my advice.

Let Tennyson's words ring clear
To follow his suggestion,
No "mourning" will we hear,
No gaiety regression.

As pains and aches increase
And spirits seem to sag,
Let not your giving cease,
Keep thankfulness your "bag."

—Richard Rathman

142

Today, Dick Rathman has found a rhyme and a reason to his life by selling others on the fact that the best possible product, the thing he believes in, is the importance of giving to others. And to think it all began when he was far beyond the age when many people consider themselves "over the hill."

Imagine you're fifty-three years old. You're a successful heart surgeon in Milwaukee, Wisconsin. Every week you are involved in up to fifteen operations. Each is risky. Most are successful. You work with some of the best-trained doctors, nurses, and technical staff, and some of the most sophisticated medical equipment in the world. Every week you walk out of the operating room and feel the deep personal satisfaction of having saved a person's life. Though the hours are long and the pressures are real, you know you've helped keep a person from dying. In some cases you've increased the person's chance to live another ten, twenty, or more years. And that's the kind of good feeling that never grows old.

But even as you rise to the peak of your profession, two things happen to shake up your career. The first is when you and your wife take a two-week trip to Kenya in the summer of 1981. There, in a remote missionary bush hospital, you see people who suffer and die because medical care comes too late or not at all. You see children and adults with congenital heart disease whose lives could be greatly improved if they could have the surgery you are trained to perform. The experience is so profound you go back to Kenya to serve short term again and again.

The second thing to happen is much more gradual and subtle. By 1988, you realize you've been in practice as a cardiac surgeon for twenty years. That translates into roughly 3,000 open-heart operations. And a very sizable income. With the money, you're able to buy a comfortable home. Later you buy a vacation home on the beach in South Carolina, then add a condo in Park City, Utah, and a mountain cabin in North Carolina. But your income also brings something else. If your name is Don Mullen, a cardiac surgeon living in Milwaukee, you remember exactly what you felt inside.

After watching my earnings increase, even though I was making more money than I reasonably knew what to do with, I was never quite satisfied. The more I acquired, the more I wanted. After I bought something new—a new car, another vacation trip with the family, a new piece of exercise equipment—I thought there was something more I had to have. I had everything I wanted, and it was *never* enough. I felt like I was on a treadmill, and I couldn't get off. The problem was *I had to get off.*

The medical work in Kenya and the medical treadmill in Milwaukee brought Don and his wife, Patsy, to a crossroads. The safe thing, the expected thing, would have been to stay another ten or fifteen years and continue doing open-heart surgery at St. Luke's Hospital. But Don had seen too much need in the world. Slowly, over time, God was operating on Don's heart. At fifty-three, feeling called to the mission field, he decided to leave the security of a three-car lifestyle in the posh River Hills area of Northside Milwaukee to attend Princeton Theological Seminary.

I've always been a person who liked to be in total control of my life. When I followed God's call to acquire the biblical training and speaking experience I needed for future, full-time ministry, I gave up control of my life. This was tough. For the next three years I had no income. Patsy and I went from living in a six-bedroom home to a one-bedroom apartment in Princeton's student housing. Besides getting used to a whole new regimen of going to classes, writing papers, and taking tests, I still had responsibilities as a husband and father. The real "capper" was that I had no job waiting for me when I graduated from seminary.

When I look at Don's decision, I see a lot of things that strike close to home in my own career as a physician. You don't have to be a doctor or a man, however, to appreciate all Don was willing to give up in order to fulfill his heart's desire:

The end to a thirty-year medical career.

The title of chief of staff at one of the largest hospitals in the Midwest.

The possible misunderstanding of colleagues who look at you and say, "You're doing *what*?"

Saying good-bye to lifetime friends from church.

The stability, security, and comfortable routine that make a place feel like home.

And then came the dreaded nightmare of having to sift through thirty years of "stuff we never use" before holding the "World's Largest Garage Sale."

Even when I imagine all that was hiding in the cup-boards of Don's three-car garage, the terror of facing all that stuff is a piece of cake compared to the real losses that come with choosing to do something daring with the rest of your life.

Making such a change was not easy for Don, and in many ways even more difficult for Patsy. "I have always been a person who likes to put down deep roots. My roots in Milwaukee were well established. I was very active in our Presbyterian Church, serving as the unofficial director of the children's education ministries. Then there was all that was involved in maintaining our home and being a mother—leaving all that we had spent so many years establishing was difficult."

A month after Don received his Master of Divinity degree from Princeton Seminary, he and Patsy were commissioned as medical missionaries by the Presbyterian Church. For two years, they traveled from one country to another, completing short-term medical mission assignments. In 1994, Don accepted the position as president of World Medical Mission, an international Christian relief ministry based in Boone, North Carolina, that places physicians, nurses, and medical support people in places of need around the world for short-term service.

"Today, we thank the Lord for calling us to live our lives in His service. It meant taking what seemed to be a giant step at the time—but Patsy and I have never looked back. We know that we made the right decision and doing so has brought us a sense of fulfillment we never could have known in our former materialistic world of money, position, and things."

When I look at Don Mullen's choice to risk his family's security to follow a call that had no clear outcome at the time, I think of something else he said, something that reminds me that courageous choices like his are not automatic.

"When I look back, I realize if I hadn't gotten off the runaway train that was running my life, I would still be in Milwaukee fighting political games at the hospital where

I worked. I would still be making a lot of money. I would still be on the treadmill, spending more time at work, less time with my family, continuing to be very driven and very unhappy."

There's an extremely thin line between staying put and striking out in a new uncharted direction. You can wander for years in the same, unsatisfying direction and not know why you're so unhappy. However, once you see an opportunity to give all that you are to all you know of God, once the need in front of you speaks to the gifts within you, and the possibilities to serve cause you to say, "What if . . . ," once these things begin to happen, the choice of what to do with the rest of your life may be easier than you think.

Like Dick Rathman, you may discover the God-given gifts and desire that cause you to say, "Yes, *this* is really who I am; *this* is really what I need to do, not out of guilt but out of love."

Like Don and Patsy Mullen, you may use your gifts in a way of serving that causes you to leave your nine-to-five-pressure-cooker world behind. Like them you may find yourself saying, "I don't know for sure what the future holds. I don't like giving up control of my life. I just know this is the right step to take."

Or like a couple named Ralph and Carolyn Furst, you may feel that you're at the end of the road. You may feel that there is no "rest of your life" to look forward to or plan. You may feel you lack the faith of a Brother Reuben or the determination of a Diane Bringgold. Though their stories are inspiring, you look at your own life and admit, "I feel like so much has been taken away, all I have left is God." This was the case with Ralph and Carolyn Furst, before their lives were completely changed.

Carolyn puts her hands on her chest and remembers when she first felt the pain.

"It was worse than childbirth," she recalls. "I almost couldn't stand it. I knew it was my heart. I just didn't know how serious it was."

Incredibly, she lived with the pain for the next three years. Finally, a doctor at UCLA Medical Center in Los Angeles revealed what Carolyn's body had been trying to tell her all along: her vital organs were dying. Her liver was enlarged and her heart was not pumping enough blood.

Over the next six years, Carolyn and her husband made so many crosstown trips to Ventura's Community Memorial Hospital they should have left a forwarding address. Carolyn began to spend more and more time in a hospital bed and less and less time convinced that things were getting any better.

After a battery of tests at UCLA Medical Center, Carolyn faced the facts. "A doctor told me I would never leave the hospital without a heart transplant. At first I was surprised. I never thought this would happen to me or that the hospital would even consider me a candidate for a new heart. The cutoff age was fifty-seven years. I was sixty-six-and-a-half. As the time for surgery got closer, I was just anxious to get done whatever needed to be done."

Carolyn held her feelings close to her own heart. Then, on April 29, 1989, she was wheeled into surgery. At the moment Carolyn's heart was experiencing cardiac arrest, another heart from a donor she would never meet was being brought down the hallway. Six and a half hours after the anesthesia began, Carolyn could feel her pulse once again. The heart of a twenty-four-year-old man was now beating inside her.

Carolyn knew she was in good company. "Ralph was by my side from eight o'clock in the morning until eight o'clock at night. When he left, God was there. We did a lot of talking. I had read the Bible. He promised that He would not give us more pain than we could handle. I believed Him. I discovered my faith was stronger when I was at my lowest.

"Because of my age, the doctors had told the cardiologist it would be a miracle if I survived." Yet, twelve days after she entered the hospital, Carolyn Furst returned to her home in Ventura. "I was so happy to have the pain gone. I just wanted to keep living."

And that she did. One Sunday during the worship service, Ralph and Carolyn noticed a man in the front pew who began to pray out loud in the middle of the sermon. "He was loud and disruptive. We learned his name was Jim. When we went over to sit with him, we found out he was mentally handicapped. We sat with him and comforted him."

Sunday mornings have never been the same since for Carolyn and Ralph. Through Jim, they got to know the men and women who lived at Lincoln Place, a home for mentally handicapped adults. "They range from nineteen to seventy-eight years old," says Ralph. "Some are bipolar; others, like Jim, suffer from Down's syndrome. We learned they are able to dress themselves and take care of themselves. But they need some help taking their medication. Mostly, they just need what we all need, to be loved."

Without trying, something new and unexpected was happening to Carolyn's heart. Her husband felt it too. "We began taking them to concerts and picnics," says Carolyn. "At first, to them, we were simply 'Carolyn' and 'Ralph.'

But it didn't take long until something began to happen. We fell in love with each one of them. We began to love them as if they were our own flesh and blood. The day they called us 'Mom' and 'Dad' they became our children."

The meaning of that realization came home one evening not long ago as the Fursts packed their suitcases for a vacation trip to Mexico.

Steve, one of our *seven kids*, always calls the night before we leave with a prayer. But the night before we left the phone didn't ring. I called Steve at eight o'clock, but he wasn't home. I waited and waited, but still no call. At ten-thirty I went to bed, but I couldn't sleep. Finally, at five o'clock in the morning, I called Steve, again. I had to talk to him. I had to hear his prayer.

"Steve," I said. "This is Mom. I'm sorry to wake you, but I missed your phone call. I miss your prayer." And then I heard the words, "Dear Lord, I love Ralph and Carolyn so much. Take them safely on their trip, and take them safely home."

Steve's prayer was answered. Today, Carolyn Furst is a woman with a new heart and a life that has new purpose.

After the transplant, I felt I had to make my life count for something. God had allowed me to live to enjoy more of life. He did that for a purpose. He led Ralph and me to these children. I didn't sit down and say, "What can I do to make my life more worthwhile?" He just led me. It was His gift to me, receiving a new heart, a new spirit of giving I didn't have before.

Facing the real possibility that her life on earth could be over, Carolyn Furst has found out what it means to live again. The only thing she's had to do is realize that God has prolonged her life for a reason. And once she knew that, she did the only thing she could—give her time, her devotion, and her heart to the people God put in her path.

One of those people is a forty-year-old woman who found herself being evaluated for a heart transplant. Out of a desire to listen, comfort, and encourage others, Carolyn called the woman, and over coffee a pair of strangers became friends. Several days after their meeting, Carolyn received a handwritten note. It read:

> *Dear Carolyn and family,*
>
> *It was such a pleasure to meet you. In a world of confusion, where strangers remain strangers, and neighbors refuse to care, a person willing to reach out in friendship, wholeheartedly as you do, is a blessing to those touched. It reminds me that it is possible to entertain angels unaware.*
>
> *From one heart to another,*
>
> *Carol Fischer*

After her operation, Carolyn could have gone back to watching television and looking out at the world through her window blinds. The easy thing would have been to turn inward and focus on her limitations. The result would have been self-pity and hopelessness. But Carolyn did the courageous thing. By giving herself to others, she met these unlikely people who taught her a great truth about true giving:

True giving—the heart of living a life that counts—starts when those we serve have nothing to give us in return. That's the snapshot of invisible reality Don and Carolyn Furst hold up. In the costly joy of sacrifice, they discovered how to make their lives count. Serving the poor, the disadvantaged, and the have-nots of our world unmasks our human motivation that asks, "What's in it for me?" Because Carolyn Furst realized there was nothing in it for her from the start, she was able to give unconditionally, without any expectation of receiving any payback in return.

You may feel incapable of doing what Ralph and Carolyn Furst have done by loving seven mentally handicapped adults over these past number of years. It doesn't matter. God is preparing and calling you (if He hasn't already!) for a time, a people, and a place especially for you. You will know it when, like Dick Rathman, you celebrate the gifts God has given you and say, "This is who I am." You will know it when, like Don Mullen, you are willing to give up control because "This is what God has called me to." And you will know the time, people, and place for giving are meant just for you when, like Carolyn Furst and Mel Cheatham, you are able to love others with a new heart.

I identify so closely with Don Mullen's experience in Kenya because what happened to him happened to me. After our family's short-term mission trip to South Korea, my world was never the same. In June of 1986, I went to Kenya, to operate on people who had never seen a doctor. Many had walked or been carried or carted from their mud-hut homes as far as fifty miles away. Never had I seen such desperate health and spiritual needs. Never had I needed to put my own life, my own daily needs, including impossible situations, out of my control and into the hands of the Great Physician. And because He gave me the strength when I felt I had nothing left inside to give, I came to give to others in His Name.

Ever since then I began to see that God, indeed, had prepared a special time, people, and place for me to serve. I remember one of those days when I became convinced of this during one of the most overwhelming, out-of-control moments I've ever faced.

In March of 1993, Sylvia and I found ourselves with ten other Christians from Samaritan's Purse in Mogadishu, the capital city of Somalia. This humid, chaotic city was a scene of total anarchy. Over the months, Mogadishu had become a tragic, lethal combination of civil war, cruel famine, and snipers who killed people at will. The horror ignited an international outcry that led to the arrival of 28,000 U.S.–led international troops, sent to restore order and assist in the distribution of food and relief supplies.

I was standing in the large, cavernous, partially bombed building in which a makeshift clinic had been set up by the medical team from Samaritan's Purse. We had been driven to this place in two military trucks, accompanied by about ten U.S. Marines to offer protection that day, since we would be working along the "Green Line." This was the invisible border between Mogadishu's two rival warlords, a place that had received some of the heaviest shelling and fiercest fighting. Once stately buildings now stood in ruins. The streets were lined with rubble and large coils of razor-sharp barbed wire.

Our "clinic" was set up in the remains of a partially bombed-out theater. The walls and roof were still largely intact, offering some element of crowd control and some protection from the hot sun.

On this day, our team of five doctors and five nurses would eventually see, examine, and treat 727 patients before the scorching midday heat, high humidity, noise,

LIVING A LIFE THAT COUNTS

flies, and hostile, unruly crowds caused us to leave. Each doctor-nurse team had an army cot on which to examine patients, a small table, and a chair. Long lines of gaunt, thinly clad Somalis of all ages waited to be seen inside the building. Outside, the streets were filled with hundreds more, trying to force their way in. The numbers were so large, the hours so short, we figured we could only spend ninety seconds with each patient!

It was about noon when I noticed a Somali man standing in the long line of people waiting to be seen by me. He was carrying a small boy about five years old. The boy's face and head were covered with flies. This usually meant infection. The awful smell of pus coming from the boy's head confirmed my hunches.

One by one I examined the patients in my line until it was the little boy's turn. My Somali helper placed the youngster on the army cot. His father, a thin, gaunt, ill-appearing man stood by and told me, through an interpreter, that his son had been "shot in the head and the right hip." The wounds were now badly infected with thick yellow pus draining out, attracting hundreds of flies like bees to honey.

"I have carried my little boy 120 miles across the desert looking for a doctor who can operate on him and save his life," said the father. "We are too tired to go any further." I knew the boy needed surgery to remove dead tissue and to drain the pus; otherwise, he would soon die from the infection.

"We have no operating room, no surgical instruments. All we have to give are pills. I don't know what more we can do," I said to the father.

"Please operate on my son, and try to save his life. You

can operate on him right here on the floor," he said. "If he dies, I can accept that, but what I cannot accept is seeing him suffering and in pain."

For a very long moment I stared into the father's tear-filled eyes, then at the little boy, then back at the father. I didn't know what to do. I didn't know what to say. In that cavernous ruin of a theater, seemingly devoid of air to breathe, I suddenly felt empty and defeated. Somehow, I had to come up with some answer for the boy's pleading father, and then get on with seeing the ever-lengthening line of patients.

"Tell the father to take his son to a place called Swedish Hospital. Perhaps it will be possible for surgery to be done there," I said to the interpreter. I had no idea what or where this hospital was but thought perhaps it would offer a place for the life-saving surgery to be done.

Outside, hundreds of sick, malnourished Somalis stood by, waiting, hoping to see a doctor. Driven by the intense midday heat, and the hot blowing wind, they were becoming difficult for even the marines to control. There was no more time to spend with this little boy. His ninety seconds were up.

The afternoon wore on, and the medications began to run low. As the sun bore down, the crowds began to clamor. The marine commander who knew the boiling mood of Mogadishu came into the building and said, "We'd better pack up quickly and get out of here. We can't control the situation much longer."

Ten quick minutes of packing our things and we were out of there. But I had one more visit to make. Several of the Samaritan's Purse nurses accompanied me to the Swedish Hospital, which proved to be a Swedish Army Mash

Unit tent hospital. It was made up of one long sausage-like tent connected to another like a giant brown caterpillar. Under its canvas roof was a series of sections: X-ray, laboratory, emergency room, operating room, and finally, rows of patient beds. This "hospital" had been set up by the United Nations forces for the sole purpose of offering medical care to U.N. troops. They might as well have had a sign on the outside that said, "Somali Patients Not Welcome."

I needed in. For the sake of the little Somali boy who required surgery, I needed to talk to someone. I started with the military guards outside and gradually worked my way up the chain of command until I was able to speak to the chief operating room nurse. She was a Swedish Army nurse who seemed more military than medical in her response.

"Please, I need to speak to the chief of surgery. There is a little boy who needs to be operated on—his father is bringing him here, and he should arrive at any moment," I said to the nurse.

Finally, the nurse called for the chief surgeon, a tall Swede with gray hair and a colonel's insignia on his military uniform. Again, I told the whole story to him. He listened politely, and then with an air of authority said, "I suppose it might be possible for surgery to be done in our hospital on a child such as you describe." Then looking down his long nose at me through the scrutinizing lower half of his bifocal glasses, he smiled weakly and said, "Unfortunately, though, it would not be possible because *we have no neurosurgeon here.*"

"Oh, yes, you do," I answered. *"I am a neurosurgeon."*

For some time the colonel stared down at me as he

searched for a proper response. I could tell he realized he had painted himself into a corner. I smiled back at him. The word that came to my mind at that moment was *"checkmate!"* I knew I had him.

Our team waited for the father carrying his son to arrive at the guard gate at the entrance of the hospital. We waited and waited, but the father and his son didn't come. After about an hour we went to our quarters, leaving word with the U.N. troops where they could find us. We waited well into the evening for a call from the Swedish Hospital telling us the little boy and his father had arrived. The call never came. When we called on our radio the next morning, we were told they never came.

I had done all I could to help. I have no doubt that God had placed me in that specific place and time to try to help this particular child who could not help himself. The fact that his father never came back didn't weaken my faith. It only heightened the fact that our team was just where we needed to be. Like Carolyn and Ralph Furst, we had been led to a place where we could help people who had nothing to give us in return. And in having nothing to offer, they offered us the most important thing of all—the chance to give with the freedom of not needing or expecting to receive anything in return.

When you find *that* kind of opportunity to serve, you won't have to worry about what to *do*. Not when you reach out like Carolyn Furst did—and let the people whom God has put in your life begin to touch you.

Before you turn the page . . .

What *tangible* sacrifices of time, money, or material possessions do you associate with the life of distinction that God is calling you to live? What *intangible* sacrifices such as security, reputation, or comfort do you risk giving up? When you think of all you might have to let go of, whom do you know who's already made a similar, risky sacrifice?

How did their possible sacrifices compare against what they learned about God's faithfulness and the unexpected joys they received by giving?

Given the possible sacrifices you've just considered, the stories your friends have shared with you, and the lives you've just read about in this chapter, what is your prayer to God?

CHAPTER NINE

The Question Jesus Will Ask You and Me Someday

The afternoon of October 8, 1993, lives inside me like a bad dream. For six anxious hours, I wondered what I had done with my life. I sat, stood, and paced inside the concrete-walled room that formed a bunker under the partially shelled airport building in Sarajevo. Cold air blew around a high wall of sandbags that was our lone protective barrier from sniper fire and shelling from the mountainside beyond and through the large broken windows. With me was a medical team of eight, including my wife, Sylvia. For fifteen days we had performed emergency surgeries on the war-wounded in the tortured land of the former Yugoslav Republic. The twelve-hour days had left us all cold, nervous, and tired. Finally, the U.N. troops instructed us to put on our flak jackets and blue metal army helmets and form a line behind the sandbags. Somewhere, out on the rain-soaked tarmac none of us could see, a United Nations transport plane had just touched down. It was our only means of escape.

Suddenly, the building shook. Not once but twice. Two mortar shells had hit.

"Run!" shouted the U.N. soldiers. One by one we tore out from behind the protective barrier and ran across the bare runway. The large Russian Ilyushin cargo plane was a hundred yards away. Two days earlier a French U.N. soldier had run across the same airstrip and had been shot and killed by a sniper. But there was no time to think. There were only seconds in which to act. There was no other option.

I don't know where you're sitting as you read this. I don't know where your life has taken you, what big decisions loom, what crossroads lie ahead, what significant steps of faith you're already living out. I don't know the prayers, doubts, questions, and convictions that live inside you as a result. Though there may be a wide gulf between the things I've experienced as a physician and the things facing you this day, I believe our lives are connected by a bridge. If you've ever chosen to help someone in a time of need, whether it's offering a stranger a ride across town, comforting a hurting friend, or giving time to the child you love—if you have done any of these things, you have stepped out onto that bridge that connects us, that bridge called "service." This chapter is where we meet on that bridge.

The fact is that you and I may have little in common when it comes to the places we've lived, the jobs we've held, and the opportunities yet to come. You'll probably never have to face the dilemma of running across an open airstrip during combat. I'll probably never have to face the hard choices confronting you this week. However, if we both claim to be followers of Jesus, if we know that our meaning, purpose, and direction are intimately tied up with Him, then our differences of work schedule and lifestyle don't really matter. One day you and I are going to leave this earth. On that day, in that moment, when we are free from our creaky human frames and stand before Jesus Christ, He is going to ask each of us one thing, **"What did you do for Me?"**

What will you say to Him?

I can't think of a greater reality check for life than this question. It's one I've asked myself many times. Did I live my life to satisfy the needs and wants of Mel Cheatham? Were my thoughts, words, and deeds motivated by wanting to serve myself or by choosing to serve others? When I did choose to serve others, did I reach out to them because of my love for Jesus? Did I love them in *His* name?

If you're serious about exploring this question, if you're committed to building a life that counts, there is great sacrifice ahead of you. There is also great joy—a joy many people don't know because the cost of giving seems too uncomfortable, too much to ask. For the first fifty-nine years of my life, I thought I knew the meaning of Christian service. And though I honestly gave myself to programs and people in the most faithful way I could, I wondered if there was something more. Then, in my sixtieth year, I saw with my own eyes the ultimate example of what it truly means to serve in Jesus' name. I experienced what it means to live a life that counts. It happened in Bosnia during the fifteen mind-numbing days that preceded my hundred-yard dash to safety. What I experienced was so deeply troubling, yet so truly inspiring, I came home a different person. I came home knowing something I had never seen before:

When you decide to serve in Jesus' name, you will find yourself in situations you never would have chosen yourself.

When you decide to serve in Jesus' name, however small your gift, wherever you go, whomever you help, two things will happen:

By giving yourself you will see and touch parts of this world's need and pain you wish you had never known. And in doing so you will be tremendously blessed.

This is the story of what it means to step across the bridge called Christian service, to be made new by giving in His name. It is not merely my story; it is the story of anyone who is moved, by love for Christ, to love others.

The request I received from Franklin Graham in September 1993 was quite simple: to organize a neurosurgical team to go to Bosnia and operate on the children, women, and men wounded by a brutal civil war. *Who would choose to leave their home in southern California and walk into a war zone?* I thought to myself as I picked up the telephone and began to call for volunteers. I did not have to look far. My wife had already popped her head in several times that Sunday afternoon, helping me plan the trip. Every time she talked about the journey she referred to "we." Finally I asked her, "What do you mean when you say '*we*'?"

"You and I," she said, "have always done everything as a team—in Korea, in Kenya, in Zaire, in Russia, and in Somalia. If you go to Central Bosnia to work, I go with you." I looked at her for a long moment, and realized our team suddenly had two members.

I phoned two surgical nurses, both good friends and committed Christians. Both had gone with us to Kenya at their own expense to care for dozens of sick villagers who needed the help our neurosurgical team could offer. "This is different," I explained to Judy Streamer and Joan Lang. "This is Bosnia, where women are being raped as an act of war, as 'ethnic cleansing.' This is a place where women and children step outside their homes and shelters and are picked off by sniper fire or exploding shell grenades."

Both Judy and Joan said, "Yes, I'll go."

"You would be stepping into a war. I can't guarantee your safety. Why don't you think about it for a couple of days." Reluctantly, they agreed. Two days later my phone rang twice. Both women gave the same response: "I told you before that I would go, and I still feel the same. I feel that the Lord is calling me to do this."

The team now numbered four. It would be impossible to do surgery without an anesthesiologist. Yet each one I asked said no. My list of possibilities had run out. Then, one morning as I was scrubbing my hands before an operation at Community Memorial Hospital in Ventura, one of the anesthesiologists, Dr. Mark Richman, came up to me.

"I hear that you're taking a neurosurgical team to Bosnia. If you need me, I'll go." After praying for days, I couldn't believe the answer. Mark Richman was very active in his Jewish temple. We would be working side by side, a Jew and a Christian, serving in a large, predominantly Muslim hospital in ethnically torn Bosnia. To the team we added Dr. Michael Van Rooyan, an emergency medical physician from Chicago, and Ivy Scarborough, a six-foot-eight-inch-tall attorney from Tennessee. Kenny Isaacs, John Clayton, and Brent Epp from Samaritan's Purse added logistical support. Though Ivy had no medical background, he believed that as a writer, the Lord could use him to tell the story of the suffering in Bosnia.

To understand the horrible killing fields that awaited our team, you need a peek back at history. And that's what Ivy helped us to do in this brief, yet telling, time capsule:

> To examine the sinister origins of the former Yugoslavia is at moments like thrusting bare hands into the putrefying cavities of a dead body to pull out organs and viscera in a repulsive effort to understand the being's growth, function, and pathologies. The history of the Balkans, the land that lies across the Adriatic from Italy, below Austria, Hungary, and Romania, and above Greece, has little to redeem it. It is a chronology of violence, invasion, and unrelenting hate, relieved only occasionally by individual acts of principle and compassion. The psychology is illustrated by an event incomprehensible to an American mind.
>
> In 1389, the Serbs were defeated at Kossovo Polje by the Turks, the start of what would be over five centuries of Ottoman domination. In 1988 the coffin of the Serbian leader killed at the battle of Kossovo Polje was taken on a tour of the country. The public display drew large crowds of black-clad mourners. Among the most vilified of the Serbian leaders today was a then relatively unknown politician named Slobodan Milosevic. He stood at Kossovo Polje and, speaking in reference to opposing Muslims and Croats, reputedly pledged: "They will never do this to you again. Never again will anyone defeat you."

Thus, out of this perverse tenacity of memory, the Serbian revolt against the Yugoslav federation began. And with it the agonies of Bosnia.

In the city of Zenica, some fifty miles southeast of Sarajevo, I experienced this long, continuing nightmare of the Balkans. In the most dire human conditions I've ever witnessed in a developed country, I saw an extraordinary example of how one person can make a difference in the lives of others. If you've ever wondered, as I have many times, what it means to serve in Jesus' name, you need only spend a moment with a man I met in Zenica's large district hospital. In the bad dream that was Bosnia, I found one person who exhibited a depth of caring I had only dreamed about.

Without knowing it at the time, of course, I was in his home of Sarajevo—the proud, picturesque city of several hundred thousand people that had hosted the 1984 Winter Olympics. Now, after eighteen months of mortar shells and sniper fire, Sarajevo was a decaying monument to suffering and death. The bodies of dead cars littered empty curbsides. Every now and then a daring man or fleeting teenager would dash through the streets clutching food to take to starving family members, who were curled up in a room with no water and no heat. This is how people survived among block upon block of partially shelled apartment buildings that showed no sign of human life. I could only imagine the fear and suffering of people trying to maintain their sanity in remains of their former homes.

The next morning, after spending the night with 600 U.N. soldiers, we were back inside armored personnel carriers on our way to Zenica. We passed through village after village of bombed and burned-out buildings. By now, the carnage and despair seemed too much. Have you ever taken the first steps in doing something you knew you were called to and then wondered out loud to yourself, "What have I done?"

These first trickles of worry are a kind of buyer's remorse of the soul. The moment we think we've gone too far, risked too much, cared too deeply, we step onto the vulnerable, fertile ground of faith. This is when the human need around us is greater than our human ability to "make it all better." This is the moment we lean most heavily on God. For me that moment came as I walked into the cracked-tile entry of Zenica Hospital, down the dark, linoleum hallways that ushered me into a feeling of outrage—and a startling new realm of grace.

I walked into the first of many hospital wards. Each had twelve beds, five along each wall and two crowded in the middle. Naked fluorescent light bulbs dangled from the ceiling. They burned only when the hospital's electric generator was running, while the rest of the city lived in darkness.

Bathed in a dim sea of cigarette smoke were the bandaged bodies and gray faces of men and women scarred by war. Their amputated stumps and silent pain screamed at me and the rest of our team. Some lay paralyzed; some remained in coma. None seemed to have any facial expression as they stared into nothingness. Most of those who were able to use their hands and breathe freely smoked cigarettes. Nicotine was the only calming companion in an ethnic hell that had killed family, friends, and a good chunk of their will to live. So many people whose bodies had been ruined by war. So many victims who had lost husbands or wives or children. So many hurting individuals who lay in silence, and yet not a single one of them ever complained.

We walked from bed to bed as the young Bosnian doctor told us what we didn't want to hear. Beyond this ward were dozens of more rooms filled with more war victims. This 600-bed hospital was filled to overflowing with 1,500 patients, most of whom were casualties of war. Caring for them were doctors paid about ten dollars per month for their work and nurses who earned about half that much.

Our purpose was to operate on patients with neurological injuries. And we did for the next fifteen days. I'm convinced, however, that when we respond to God's call to serve, we discover another purpose that is perhaps more significant than our original "job description." That reason began to unfold literally before my eyes each day at Zenica Hospital. By the second or third day, the attitude of the patients began to change. When we opened the door to a crowded ward, men and women broke into smiles and began to wave back. Some of the women blew kisses of appreciation. Just our presence had made a difference. It was only a prelude to the difference one special person made in my life.

His name was Dr. Josip Jurisic. Though his home was Sarajevo, he had been deployed to Zenica Hospital by his superiors because the hospital had no neurosurgeon to care for the war victims. Imagine a 1,500-bed hospital in your own city in the midst of a bloody two-year-old civil war. Imagine your husband, wife, child, or best friend needing surgery to remove fragments of bullets and bone from their brain or pieces of shrapnel from their spine, knowing that if the operation weren't performed, your loved one would almost certainly die. Imagine being the only person trained to do such an operation in hospital conditions that resembled those of the 1940s in America. Imagine having to perform this surgery amidst thunder of exploding mortar and cannon shells and frequent generator power failures. This was Dr. Josip's daily challenge.

Going to the hospital each day meant risking one's life.

LIVING A LIFE THAT COUNTS

During one period of ten days we had no running water in the hospital. There was no way to wash surgical scrub suits, so we operated in our undershirts. Since we had no way to wash and sterilize surgical drapes, we had to operate without any. Ordinarily, we would have feared infections developing under such conditions, but in war everything becomes relative to everything else. Just stopping the bleeding and trying to close wounds and amputate limbs was the first priority. We didn't even have water to wash our hands between operations.

Dr. Josip was a man who had put his safety, his life calling, and his destiny in the hands of God. As a follower of Jesus, Dr. Josip believed the Lord accompanied him in whatever he faced and wherever he went. He displayed a level of faith I have rarely seen, a depth of conviction that had been tempered by tragedy and trust. In slightly broken English he told his story to me. In a small room where we would not be overheard, he flashed back to the hospital in Sarajevo where he had worked during the first one-and-a-half years of the war.

This was a man who had lost sixty-two pounds over the previous eighteen months because he didn't have enough to eat. This was a man who, just after completing his neurosurgical training, was thrust into doing endless operations under nearly impossible conditions. When he told me of the numbers of neurosurgical cases he had operated on at Kosovo Hospital in Sarajevo, I was both astonished and filled with admiration. When he told me his personal story, my heart was filled with compassion.

Dr. Josip showed me a crinkled photograph he carried in his wallet. It was of a young woman and a small boy. "This is a picture of my wife and son taken when we were still together," he said. Then, he carefully unfolded a yellowed newspaper photograph showing him saying a final good-bye to his wife and son as they were being evacuated by bus from Sarajevo early in the war, because there was too much fighting for them to stay any longer. The photograph showed Dr. Josip standing alongside the bus with his hand against the outside of the window. It was pressed against the outstretched hand of a son on the inside who wanted, one more time, to touch his daddy. At that moment they were separated by only a pane of glass, a separation Josip realized might be for the rest of their lives.

Dr. Josip's voice cracked as he recalled the scene. I looked again at the wrinkled photograph and knew why. "I waited in the cold a few more minutes," he said. "My pregnant wife and son waved, and I waved. Then the crowded bus drove away and that was it. For the next few days, I went back to the hospital to work and tried to forget what had happened. I thought in a month, perhaps two months, I would hear from them, or at least learn their whereabouts."

The news came much sooner, however. Several days after he had waved good-bye, Dr. Josip called the telephone number in Dubrovnic where he believed his wife and son were. As the dial tone buzzed in his ear, he wondered about his wife's health. She was near term with their next child and her blood pressure had been running very high. He just wanted her safe, and well, and home in his arms.

After several rings, he heard a voice on the other end. It was his son with words he couldn't believe.

"Daddy, Daddy, I think Mama has died." Without another sentence, without any time to think, or question, or ask his son to please say more, the line went dead. "I was so overwhelmed with sadness and worry and grief, I thought it impossible to go on, yet, I had no other option. At the hospital the number of casualties was unending. I had no choice but to keep going, and to keep praying for my wife, my son, and the baby that may or may not have existed.

"Then, after many days, I got the word: my wife had nearly died in childbirth, but finally she had survived. Her condition was still very bad. She had given birth to a baby girl! Our son was well! Every day I thanked God for His many blessings to me and my family. That day, and every day, I thanked God for the child I longed to see and hold in my arms."

I tried to imagine myself in Dr. Josip's shoes and enduring all he had shared. Some might call his courage a testimony to the strength of the human spirit, but I prefer to call it a tribute to the faithfulness of God.

Over the next fifteen days, Dr. Josip, our Samaritan's Purse team, and I operated on many patients. No doubt each would have died without successful surgery. Nothing can minimize the value of helping to save a person's life. Yet the deeper reason for being in Bosnia was the Croatian doctor who walked into my life and changed my heart without knowing it. We had just finished our last operation at Zenica Hospital. As we were leaving the operating room, Dr. Josip asked, "Professor, can I have your dress?"

"I would be glad to give it to you. That way we can write letters after the war is over and keep in touch."

"No, no, no," he said. "I don't mean your address, I mean your dress." He then pointed to my sweaty, blood-splattered, surgical scrub suit. "I would be very honored to have the surgical clothing which you have worn while you've operated here in Zenica. If I might have this, it would bring great honor to me, to wear the same garments which you have worn."

A feeling of deep humility came over me. This man genuinely felt honored to have a rumpled, soiled garment to wear in his upcoming surgeries. Surely, surgical suits like mine were a rare and valued commodity in Bosnia. But the rarer commodity that Dr. Josip treasured was the friendship we had formed. I was just one person in his life. Though I was a foreign visitor who had come from the other side of the world to help, though I was a fellow neurosurgeon able to impart a handful of medical knowledge in the brief time we spent in surgery, though we experienced the fellowship of Christians committed to following Christ, I was just one person among other much more important people in Dr. Josip's burdened life. To think of what he carried around inside of him:

To not know if your wife is alive.

To not have seen or held your newborn child.

To not be sure if your patients or your homeland will survive another week.

With all this going on inside him, Dr. Josip made me feel as if I were the only person that mattered. He cared deeply for me as a person. I believe I know the reason why. This man so thin of bone, so big of heart, had so filled himself with the compassion of Jesus that demonstrating the love of Jesus came naturally. Serving others, as he had served me, came without hesitation. Dr. Josip's love had grown for years not because of what he *believed* about Jesus, or solely what he *read* about Jesus; his contagious, visible love was real and alive because of what he *did* to serve others, including myself, just as Jesus would have had *He* been operating in a battle zone.

Dr. Josip always went ahead of me to open doors to hospital corridors or patient rooms, that I might freely pass through. Though we didn't have much food to eat when we paused between surgeries twice each day, he would always serve me first. On several occasions, he came to our team's living quarters in the dark of night to see that we were doing well. I must assume that he walked the several miles through dangerous unlit streets in freezing cold.

Dr. Josip showed me that regardless of how inadequate I felt about myself, or how powerless I felt to act, God could use me to make a difference in the lives of others. I had come to Bosnia thinking, *Six centuries of bitterness, rekindled revenge, and thousands of cruel and needless deaths are too much to handle. What can I do to change things? The need is too big, and I'm too small to make any meaningful difference.*

Why do so many Christians feel this way? Why are there people like you and me who feel called to serve, who want to serve but don't know where to start, or who feel so discouraged even though they're already actively serving in His name? Lots of Christians (myself included) approach their own Bosnias wanting to change the world. I went to Bosnia and had my world changed by a buoyant, emaciated gentleman who taught me a lesson:

When you serve others in Jesus' name, all He asks is that you touch one person.

For years I had heard this truth. In Dr. Josip I met one person who *lived* this truth. I came to Bosnia to serve, unprepared to meet the *one* who would serve *me* in the most selfless manner. Isn't it ironic that when we feel we are unable, or unwilling, to give or we think we can't give any more, God places a Dr. Josip in our path who is more needy, more helpless than we are. Amazingly he or she gives to us more generously and effortlessly than we could ever imagine. This person serves with tenderness and endurance in Jesus' name because he or she isn't living for self. Since such people no longer need to protect their images or their egos, they're free to give to *one person at a time*. If you've been that one person on the receiving end then you know the world *does* change. It changes because of God now at work in people like you. Your world changes because if the love you've received is truly from God, it is impossible for you to keep it to yourself! In this way you're truly free to love others.

The freedom of knowing that all God calls us to do is to serve one person at a time prepared me for a second invaluable lesson about what it means to serve in Jesus' name.

It happened seven miles behind enemy lines in Nova Bila, a small enclave of 18,000 Croat people in a valley completely surrounded by the Bosnian Muslim Army. A former Catholic monastery and church had been converted into the village's lone hospital, and two rooms in the basement had been made into an operating room. A third room functioned as a morgue. It was the sanctuary, though, that grabbed my heart. Originally designed for worship, it had become a last-ditch-effort home to ninety war casualties. In some cases pews had been turned facing each other to serve as beds. Stretched out on these cold wooden rows were the victims of war. Other patients lay in antiquated iron hospital beds.

At the front of the sanctuary, a wooden image of Christ on the cross hung above the altar, still in place, still set for Holy Communion. In a far corner stood a massive, metal potbellied stove with a large, rusty stovepipe running out through a hole in the roof. With the indoor temperature hovering in the thirties, what a gift this was for the two patients who stood with their hands outstretched, nearly touching the stove. The strange, sad fact however, was that there was no fire in the stove. No wood, no coal, no heat. It was stone cold! These patients could only stand there and pretend they were receiving warmth to take the chill off the room's bitter air.

As we made rounds, moving from bed to bed, we saw the carnage of war, people of all ages who had been horribly shot up. Sylvia and I came to the bed of a young Croat man in his twenties. It didn't occur to me that he might speak English. "Both of my hands were blown off," the young man said. "When a live grenade was thrown into our home, I picked it up with both hands to try to throw it away from family members. It exploded in my hands." When I looked into his eyes, I saw another young man about the same age—my son, Robert.

"We have a son who is about your age. He looks much like you. Would you mind if my wife and I had our photo taken with you?" I asked.

"I would be honored," he said. "But my body has not been bathed or my teeth brushed for over two weeks. You may not want to stand near me." Here was a young man apologizing to us for his condition. The tragedy of everything I had seen that morning suddenly got to me. They say grown men aren't supposed to cry, but I couldn't help it. Standing there, not wanting to leave this young man's bedside, I felt an overwhelming desire to help him in some way. I would have given anything to have been able to restore even one of his hands. With tear-filled eyes we both smiled and a silent message passed between us. I patted him on the shoulder and said, "God bless you, son. I hope we meet again someday."

I, along with the rest of the team members, had tears in my eyes and prayers on my lips as we made our way through the labyrinth of hospital beds and patients. I knew it would be impossible to reach all of these people. But I could reach one. Within a minute I had found that person.

He was a young Croat soldier whose head was wrapped in bandages. The truck he had been driving was riddled with 150 machine-gun holes. One of these bullets had partially blown away his left shoulder. Another had penetrated deep into his brain, leaving him motionless, partially paralyzed, and comatose.

"He will die if he isn't operated on," I told Bruno, our interpreter. "It is not possible for our team to perform the operation now since we have to return across the enemy lines to Zenica Hospital to perform surgery there. If the British Battalion soldiers will bring us back tomorrow, we can operate on this man—if he is still alive then." I knew waiting a day wasn't good, but we really had no choice.

In the darkness of the following morning, we did return to Nova Bila. Bruno led our neurosurgical team down the stairs of the rectory. Behind a protective barrier of sandbags and slanting, thick timbers we came into the makeshift operating room. Mark Richman started the general anesthetic that would cause the patient to sleep. During the seven minutes required for scrubbing our hands I felt very privileged to be in this place to help save a young man's life. Everything in the room seemed so vivid: The low concrete ceiling, the whitewashed concrete walls, and the old operating table and surgical equipment made everything seem like a strange dream.

As I looked around at the people on our team who were poised for the surgery to start, I hesitated for an instant. A few days before leaving for Bosnia, I had awakened in the middle of the night. My heart was racing. Something terrible had happened. A nightmare! Without thinking it started all over again . . .

> *The time had come for us to leave Bosnia.*
>
> "Mel, the airplane engines are running. It's time to leave. We've got to go!" Ken Isaacs, the project director, was insistent. "Hurry, we've got to go, or there's no way out of here!"
>
> At that moment, the Bosnian nurses brought in another child. He had been shot in the head by a sniper. Without immediate attention he would die.

The dream was so real, the dilemma so traumatic. I lay awake the rest of the night with a scene that wouldn't leave me alone. It all came back as I stood at the small sink scrubbing my hands. Silently I prayed that God would work through our team despite the few supplies and surgical instruments we had to work with.

Dr. Kulic, the Nova Bila surgeon, and Sylvia assisted me. He had already applied iodine solution to the scalp. I covered all but the scalp surrounding the gaping wound in the head with sterile green sheets. I stood for a moment longer than I usually would reviewing the operative procedure in my mind one more time, not knowing what it would mean to the surgeon who stood on my left in a few hours.

The entire medical staff of eleven doctors and nurses had crowded into the small operating room to observe the operation. It wasn't curiosity that pulled them away from their other urgent work. They were here to take a one-hour crash course in brain surgery. They knew that before our neurosurgical team arrived, many patients with sniper bullets or shrapnel wounds of the brain had died in their beds at Nova Bila. What they would learn from watching this operation might save the lives of others.

Every step I performed they had to commit to memory:

Removing the damaged scalp, hair, dirt, and old blood deep in the wound.

Enlarging the scalp wound to free things up enough to close after completing the brain work. Then biting away the edges of the fractured skull and seeing dead brain tissue start to protrude.

Now going deeper into the brain, removing blood clots and pieces of skull bone and bullet fragments.

Watching the brisk, bright bleeding start.

Trying to control it without proper neurosurgical instruments.

Then taking a one-inch-diameter piece of fascia lining from the outside of the skull and sewing it in place to cover over the deep cavity in the brain.

Finally, suturing the six-inch-long wound of the scalp back together.

Then, the operation was completed.

In a little while, Dr. Richman had the young Croat soldier awakening from the anesthetic. The operation had been a success so far. Our team only had fifteen minutes left before the British Battalion would arrive to take us back across enemy lines to Zenica. Just enough time for some very black coffee and watery bean soup, and to exchange smiles at the table with Dr. Kulic and the other local doctors.

Then it happened. My nightmare became a reality.

Dr. Anika, the young, female Bosnian doctor, rushed into the room holding a blurry X ray. Her broken English spilled out. "Come, please. Please, you must see one more patient, a seventeen-year-old boy. He's just been shot in the head by a sniper's bullet."

Quickly, I followed Dr. Anika into the large church, passing rows of wounded patients, finally arriving at the bedside of the young boy. It was nasty. The entrance wound was in his forehead and there was an exit wound at the rear of his scalp on the right side. Every few seconds, damaged brain matter oozed out of his head due to the pressure building up inside.

I looked at Dr. Anika and Dr. Kulic. "He needs to be operated on right away. We need to do the same operation we just performed on the other patient." Then the bad news: their only means of sterilizing surgical instruments was in a pressure cooker over a wood fire. "It will require one and a half hours to get the instruments ready again," Bruno said.

I raced back upstairs to the rectory room and found Ken Isaacs.

"Mel, the Brit Bats are here to get us. They're nervous about getting us out of here. Get your flak jacket and helmet on. We've got to leave right now—the engines are running!"

"Kenny, there's a young boy, shot through the head. We

need to operate on him." I looked around the room at our team in their flak jackets and helmets, ready to go. Even as I heard my own words, I knew we had to leave. I could hear my heart pounding and feel a large lump in my throat. My nightmare had come to life.

I had only one option. Only one person could do the operation, and it wasn't me. I found Dr. Kulic, then found Bruno, and sat them down at a table. Then, I drew a picture of the wounded boy's head. In simple step-by-step narration, I described to Dr. Kulic the operation he had seen me perform a short time before—the same operation he would now do. The entire surgery, every step needed to remove bone, bullet fragments, and blood clots from the brain of a teenage boy who now clung to life was passed from me to Bruno, then to Dr. Kulic. We had no anatomy books, no opportunity to speak in words we both understood. Dr. Kulic's nods and smiles, along with his assurances that reached me in Bruno's broken English, were the only assurances I had that things would be all right.

British Battalion Captain Mark Hancock appeared in the doorway. He nervously clutched his automatic rifle. "Come on now, we must go quickly before the darkness," he said. Snapping the olive drab canvas strap of my Kevlar™ helmet under my chin as I walked, I followed him to the back of the waiting white Land Rover with "U.N." painted on the sides. The others were already inside as the door was slammed behind me. Looking out through the mud-covered rear window, I saw Dr. Kulic, Dr. Anika, Dr. Bruno, the parish priest, and several nurses waving farewell. I wondered what would happen to these brave people and whether we would ever meet again.

Then we were gone. In less than a minute the nervous

British soldiers had whisked us away from Nova Bila. Faster than I imagined, the sky turned black. Every mile on the way back to Zenica I thought of Dr. Kulic. I envisioned him and the team carefully, methodically taking the bullet fragments out of the teenage boy. As we bounced along, swerving around muddy curves, passing villages reduced to ruin by mortar shells, I operated in my mind with Dr. Kulic. I could see him completing each step of the procedure just as I had shown him several hours before. I could see them being a success. I could see this young boy's life being saved, just like the soldier on whom I had operated earlier. But this time, I hadn't lived a nightmare, I had awakened to a truth:

When you are freed to serve in Jesus' name, all He asks is that you give all that you have and all that you are to that one person He puts before you.

For years I had tried to follow Jesus as if I were sprinting a marathon. I would go from project to project, phone call to follow-up meeting, always hurrying up to wait, always falling behind. I thought picking up Paul's banner to "run the race set before you" would make me an extremely effective, productive, and therefore fulfilled Christian. But all my constant running really did was make me feel out of breath.

The problem with being busy for God is that there's never a finish line. When you're done, you're never really done! What happened to the words, "Well done, good and faithful servant"? They were lost and buried under the sea of Post-it notes that remind you of the phone calls you forgot to return, the people you didn't have time to see because you said yes to God.

The risk of stepping out and serving, of saying yes to God, is that you'll race, huffing and puffing, toward an invisible finish line, confessing one of two things:

"God has given me too much!" or "I can't do it all; it's too much for one person."

My nightmare in Bosnia was that I wouldn't get everything done in time. And I didn't! Had I thought that God had called me to train a large number of doctors in Central Bosnia I might have missed the one person He had placed in my life at that time, the one person He was calling me to serve, Dr. Kulic. When I had to leave Nova Bila, he was the one person who could do the neurosurgery and save the life of the young Croat soldier. All I could give Dr. Kulic was all that I knew and all that I had. Even though I felt inadequate, even though I wanted to do more, "all" was enough.

You and I can't serve an entire country, a city, or even a group all at once. But we *can* serve *one* person. Serving *one person* allows us to give all that we have and all that we are in His name. Serving *one* person at a time gives us a realistic finish line we can see and run toward with confidence. Perhaps the greatest "prize" is knowing that you may not be the one to cross that finish line. I couldn't help save the life of the young Croat soldier. That privilege was left to Dr. Kulic.

This month, this week, *today*, God may place a Dr. Kulic in *your* life. Before your truck leaves, God will give you a certain amount of time so that you can give another person the gift of yourself, a gift of wisdom, direction, or encouragement he or she needs, a gift only *you* can give. All that you have and all that you are is all you need to touch another's life before it's time for you to leave.

And when we've done all that we can, the question all of us ask and want to know is, "Did I make a difference?" The only answer I can offer is wrapped up in the story that defined the terrible beauty of Bosnia and showed me a third revealing truth of what it means to serve in Jesus' name.

At six o'clock in the afternoon on our first day at Zenica Hospital, I was standing over the operating table removing a sniper's bullet from the cervical spinal cord of a soldier when news reached us of a new patient. As Dr. Josip closed up the gaping neck wound, Mark Richman and I went to examine this new arrival. We had only sixty minutes left before the seven o'clock wartime curfew, hardly time to operate on another patient. But when I saw this little girl, I knew we had no other choice.

Her name was Raza. She was probably no more than ten years old. A bloody bandage hung loosely just below her blonde hair. She was a beautiful child in excruciating pain. Thanks to Dr. Rasim, who could speak some English, I found out the awful reason. One hour earlier, on a rare sunny afternoon, her mother sent her and her little brother to another house in their village in search of some bread because the family had no food. Normally, the air would have been cold and damp. With the sun out, however, the world felt comparatively warm, the village calm. For once there had been no enemy shelling for several hours.

Somewhere between her home and the neighbor's front door the stillness stopped. Raza never saw it coming, never heard the explosion of the shell grenade, never had time to cry for help. Killing or maiming children had become one of the cruelest strategies in Bosnia. Soldiers on both sides knew that crippling children was the most effective way to dishearten their enemies, to cause them to give up and move. When I looked at Raza, I found this barbarous logic almost too much to take.

A large grenade fragment had lodged in the back of her neck, fracturing her spine and paralyzing her from the shoulders down. Another fragment had ripped into her back between the shoulder blades coming to rest in her chest near her left lung. I had no doubt that without surgery she would join the thousands of children already killed in Central Bosnia. When I got to her bed she was lying on her back looking up. As our anesthesiologist, Mark Richman, remembers, "Her wide hazel eyes were looking far away in a fog of shock." In those precious few moments that precede surgery, thanks to Mark, I learned about this little girl who would never be able to tell me her own story.

In a more peaceful time, before her homeland exploded in hatred, Raza must have loved to ride her bike along the Bosnia River that gently works its way through Zenica. She had the tall, slender build of a long-distance runner or perhaps a ballerina. Now she weighed only sixty pounds. Though she was ten, the past eighteen months of near starvation in her city had caused her to shrivel until she had the body of an eight- or nine-year-old girl.

This lovely, innocent child had endured not one but two shrapnel wounds. It was after 9:00 P.M. when we finished the operation. Mark then took her to the ward and laid her in a bed between a sniper victim shot in the head and an elderly woman who had suffered a skull fracture when hit by the butt of a soldier's rifle. Though Raza's eyes were open, though she had made it through surgery, though we had made it back to our quarters despite the curfew, I didn't sleep well that night.

Over the days that followed, though Raza remained paralyzed, some sensation returned in her legs. Each day Sylvia, Joan Lang, and Judy Streamer would visit her and try to get her to speak or to smile, but Raza never did. There was no longer anything in the life of this little girl for her to smile about. The last time I saw Raza she still lay motionless, looking up but not appearing to register what she saw. I wondered what would happen to her. I wondered if I would ever find out.

I was still thinking about her fifteen days later when I, with the rest of our team, was minutes from leaving Sarajevo Airport for Zagreb and the flight home. We stood there in the bunker and when the mortar shells hit nearby the cry went up: "Run!" There was nothing between us and the plane but one hundred yards of dark, wet, naked runway. With Sylvia just ahead of me where I could see her, we ran. Ran like there was no tomorrow. Ran with the soundtrack of war in our ears. Ran until our boot soles struck the metal flooring of the open tail ramp of the U.N. transport plane. A soldier gave Sylvia a shove and she literally fell against the cold metal as I struggled to hold her up.

Five days later I was home in Ventura. Home to a warm bed, home to safe, familiar routines like bringing in the mail. That's how I heard about Raza. She had died a few days after we left Zenica Hospital from pneumonia brought on by her weakened condition and the paralysis that kept her from being able to breathe deeply enough to expand her lungs.

I had come home to the question that had stalked me in the shadows of my doubts: Did I make a difference? Did I *really* make a difference?

Strangely enough, Raza's death allowed me to come "home" to a new reason to keep following Jesus, to keep serving others in His name—and to keep risking. A long time ago, I let go of the expectation that making a difference was synonymous with keeping someone alive. Often in my work, despite my best efforts and the Herculean attempts of colleagues more able than I, death won out. There is nothing more humbling and defeating than to have a patient die even though you have done everything humanly possible to save him or her.

Though death robbed Raza of this life, it didn't rob Sylvia and me and Dr. Mark Richman who administered the anesthesia, and Judy and Joan who stroked her blonde bangs, and any of the five other members of our Samaritan's Purse team of the opportunity to care. Death can take away the person you love, but it cannot take away the person you *are*. I believe when Jesus puts one person in your path, one person to whom you can give all that you have and all that you are, you may fall short of your goal. Your patient, your expectations may come up short of what *you* thought would happen. Discouragement over the *results* of giving can bruise your heart, but it won't stop it from beating or from caring again for one other person once more. In the selfless Christian servants from Bosnia I saw a stark yet beautiful snapshot of a reality come into focus:

When you serve in Jesus' name, not even death—or whatever defeat looks like—can rob you of your reason for serving God who is at work in you.

Risking death, defeat, loss, or disappointment is not the kind of thing you and I are all that wild about. It's not the kind of teaser or lead-in that's apt to sell many books! But risking *is* the ultimate consequence for anyone who believes there is something more to life than wondering, "What's in it for me?"—who becomes a follower of Jesus, who seeks to lead a life that counts. If you seek to be that kind of person, then the last and final chapter of our journey may surprise you.

Before you turn the page . . .

What ultimate risk—potential disappointment, fear, defeat—is holding you back from taking the next step forward to serve others in Jesus' name? It may be a past experience or encounter or an imagined fear.

Whatever it is, picture laying it in Jesus' outstretched hands. What does He say to you? What do *you* say to *Him?*

Suppose He were to tell you that, even though you may experience hardship, nothing you can do or say by serving others in His name would diminish who you are as a person or as His child.

How do Jesus' words to you in this exercise, how does His Word of assurance to you in Romans 8:38–39, change how you look at the risky opportunities before you?

CHAPTER TEN

The Life That Truly
Counts . . .
in Twenty-five Words

One piece of paper, a crayon, and twenty-five words. These were the only materials the retreat leader told us we could use. The assignment was equally simple.

I want you to think about your life. I want you to think about what you've done with the years God has given you. I want you to think about the time that still lies ahead of you. Someday that time is going to end. Someday you're going to die. People are going to come to your memorial service, and they're going to say things about you. What do you want them to say? When your life is over, how do you want to be remembered? This is your epitaph. How do you want it to read? You've probably not done a whole lot of thinking about your own epitaph. That's why I'm going to give you the chance to write it, right now. You have twenty-five words and ten minutes. When your life is over, how do you want to be remembered?

The epitaph for American culture in the 1990s is spoken

fluently by millions: "I'll do it tomorrow." Filling out income tax forms can wait till tomorrow. Vacuuming can wait till tomorrow. Reading the Bible can wait till tomorrow. Playing with the children can wait till tomorrow. Living can wait till tomorrow.

I learned the definition of "tomorrow" thirty-three years ago from Sergeant "Tommy" Thomas, a medical corpsman who served with me in the Air Force. He was about five feet, ten inches tall, muscular and good-looking. Most of all he was confident. In the base hospital emergency room, he was the first line of defense for people who had an illness, stepped on a piece of broken glass, or had been hit by a car. Though he lacked a doctor's depth in medical knowledge, he was a whiz at applying what he knew, and I had great respect for him. I knew how to set broken bones, for instance. But when it came to applying a plaster cast, my efforts paled in comparison to Sergeant Thomas's.

More than his skill, I admired his character. He had a genuine politeness and respect for others. It was always "Yes, sir" and "Yes, ma'am." For him courtesy was more than military formality, it was a true sign of our growing friendship. I knew I could count on him, and he knew he could call on me. One fall afternoon, for instance, Sergeant Thomas had called me to the emergency room three separate times. By the time his duty shift ended at 4:00 P.M., I knew he was tired. I watched him walk past the blue Air Force ambulance to his car and looked forward to seeing him the next morning when he'd come back on duty.

Ten minutes later I was in a surgical ward seeing patients when I heard the emergency page over the intercom: "Captain Cheatham, Captain Cheatham! Please report to the emergency room. STAT!" I bolted down the stairway. In less than half a minute, I reached the emergency room entrance to see medics unloading the ambulance. On the stretcher lay Sergeant Thomas. His face and forehead were cut up. He was pale but fully conscious. It was obvious breathing was very painful for him.

It can't be him, I thought to myself. *This was the man I was working with just minutes ago. Maybe this is a drill, and they are using him as the patient.*

"Sorry, Dr. Cheatham," he said, "I didn't get very far before having a little accident." As he struggled to talk, I hurried alongside the ambulance cart into the emergency room. Sergeant Thomas had turned left on the narrow two-lane highway next to the base. Less than a mile later he met a speeding pickup truck trying to pass another vehicle on a hill. They crashed head-on. In those days, seat belts were a rarity. Sergeant Thomas's body slammed full force against the steering wheel; his face had hit the windshield.

Still, he tried to talk. "Sir, I have a terrible pain in my chest. It really hurts to breathe," he said. I couldn't work fast enough to cut open the blue uniform and shirt of my colleague and friend. His pain was increasing. Though his anterior chest wall was badly bruised, he didn't appear to have any obvious major injuries. I thought we had a chance. We got two IVs started and hooked up an EKG machine to monitor his heart.

After a quick exam and recording his vital signs and making sure they were stable, we wheeled him across the hallway for some X rays. As we lifted Sergeant Thomas onto the X-ray table I could tell his breathing was now more labored. His blood pressure was falling fast and his face was growing more pale.

Suddenly, he reached for my left wrist and gripped it tightly. "Doc, I'm not going to make it. Please don't let me die." Struggling for air, he almost willed the words out of his mouth: "I'm going to die!" At that moment, the grip on my wrist loosened and his eyes rolled back. He had lost consciousness. I looked at the EKG monitor and saw a straight line. Sergeant Thomas had suffered a cardiac arrest.

There are moments in life, particularly in a doctor's life, when actions become automatic, when thinking and doing become one. For me, this was one of those moments. As my general surgical colleague, Whitney White, inserted a tube down Sergeant Thomas' throat to create an airway and a means of breathing for him, I knew what had to happen. In those days before closed cardiac massage there was only one way to get a heart beating again.

A corpsman had just pulled the red emergency cart alongside the table. "Gimme the knife," I yelled to him. With a single, uninterrupted movement I made the long slash across Sergeant Thomas's left chest wall. Then I reached inside to massage his heart. His chest cavity was filled with so much blood, I couldn't even see his lung. I took his heart in my hand and began to rhythmically squeeze it. It was limp and motionless. While I continued the cardiac massage, Whit White squeezed the ventilation bag to pump air and oxygen into Sergeant Thomas's lungs. Two nurses and three corpsmen scurried to hang bottles of blood which poured full speed into his veins.

Suddenly, the warm blood which bathed my right hand and wrist became cold.

It can't be. We can't lose him, I thought to myself. *It can't be . . .*

But we kept going. As my heart raced, the heart of my friend remained limp. The EKG monitor showed no electrical activity. The anesthetist reported no blood pressure. Whit reported no pulse. By now Sergeant Thomas's pupils were widely dilated. This muscular man in blue military dress uniform lay still.

"He's gone," said Whit.

I loosened my hand from around Sergeant Thomas's heart, then paid attention to what my own heart was trying to tell me.

No, this can't be, I thought. *It can't be.*

I looked up at the face of the large clock on the wall. It was 4:28 P.M. Thirty minutes ago a person had been smiling and laughing, looking forward to tomorrow. Now he lay dead.

In a handful of minutes *your* life could change forever in ways you haven't realized.

Like Pat Chaney, the schoolteacher whose students walk across the street each week to help tutor handicapped students, you could look outside your window and realize that the opportunity to make a difference in someone's life is closer than you think.

Like Brother Reuben, the young Bible school student from Texas who prayed, "Lord, send me to a place no one else is able to go, a place no one is willing to go," you could discover your own unique place of service in a quiet prayer that only God can hear.

Like Jerry and Dee Miller, the couple who never imagined they'd turn their backs on the challenges and rewards of corporate America, you could get a phone call about an opportunity to serve others that was so ideally suited to your gifts and calling that you said, "Why shouldn't I do this?"

Like Dean Miller, the warm, coffee shop pastor who introduced a retired business executive to an alcohol and drug rehabilitation center, you could discover that serving the one person God puts in your path is the most effortless, natural thing you've ever done.

If you were to get to know each of these people, as I have, it would only take you a handful of minutes to see that Pat, Reuben, Jerry, Dee, and Dean are bursting inside with life. You would feel an unmistakable genuineness and integrity that admits to real human hopes and disappointments. I suspect it wouldn't take long, as has happened with me, before you would look at each of these people and find yourself saying, "Your life has meaning. I can tell, because you're at peace with who you are. What happened? What made you the person you are today?"

Then, they would share with you from the heart. They would recall the new, unfolding personal discoveries they've made about the God who is at the center of the stories you've read in this book. You would hear the refreshing candid confessions of people who found themselves sailing along in life. They would tell you that something began to happen. The scenery got boring somehow, they lost their bearing and began to drift. One day they realized they were without an anchor, so the only thing left to do was keep moving ahead faster and more furiously in life, even though they knew they were lost.

Then, these changed people would tell you about the day a new wind began to blow and how, by going with its power, a different kind of journey began, one that would define the rest of their lives. And the thing that made life so different from their previous existence as carefree drifting sailors is that they discovered where their only source of power lay. They discovered that they were nothing without the wind.

Have you ever stopped to consider this unseen power that's allowed you to stay afloat all these years? Have you been content to merely breeze along in life and take the wind for granted? Or do you think it's possible that within a handful of months, or weeks, or days, your direction could change? Could the unseen love of God that's allowed these people to chart a new life course of serving others guide you to a new, meaningful destination?

The answer depends a lot on whether you're willing to untie from the dock and set sail for somewhere you've never been. Living a life that counts means admitting that we human beings long for a safe harbor. As human beings with protective, fearful natures, we long for the security and comfort of a home port, a sanctuary from life's storms, a familiar place where we can moor our frayed nerves and ride out life's inclement gusts.

Living a life that counts also means recognizing that, as human beings, we were meant to journey. Harbors are only temporary shelter, a chance to refuel. The real adventure takes place out on the open water. You and I weren't created to remain in dock and let barnacles collect. We were created to sail, and the only way I know to do that is to be willing to trust our lives to God who will guide us to the people He's prepared for us to meet and serve. If you are willing to set sail, if you are open to let God take you on a new journey, I'm convinced a great adventure lies ahead for you beyond your safe and present harbor.

The people in this book will tell you they didn't just cut their ropes, cast off from the dock, and sail willy-nilly. They spent much time preparing for their journeys by refining their skills. Each person would tell you that the most important navigational tool they studied for years, the Map that became their compass, anchor, and the only accurate chart they could trust, was the Bible. And yet when everything was ready, every one of the people in this book who have sailed a life that counts will tell you that the real journey began when they pushed off from the dock.

How does one do that? In March of 1992, I met Rolly Laing. For over twenty-three years he had been a very successful trial attorney in Calgary, Alberta, Canada. At breakfast one day, he told me the story of how he had loosened the lines on all that tied him and his wife, Pam, to a secure, yet not totally fulfilling existence. He told me how they had pushed off from the safe harbor of his own profession. As he recounted the speech he had given to his firm, I thought, *How many other people, other than high-flying attorneys, would be able to identify with this man?* Instantly I knew the answer: *A lot of people!* Though few might appreciate the unique stresses and strains of Rolly's specialized career, it struck me that virtually anyone could identify with his words.

It's interesting how we work together for years and learn so little about each other. We tend to be satisfied with sharing the moment and avoid, or at least miss, opportunities to really understand each other's hearts. Some have called it the trauma of transparency.

Sometimes, however, circumstances develop which call for, or at least permit, the sharing of personal aspects of life, things which would normally be closely held. In the next few minutes, I want to risk transparency by sharing with you some of the details of how I came to my decision to leave the firm.

Growing up in the home of a Baptist pastor, I saw in my father a passionate commitment to a single theme. It's expressed in the third chapter of the gospel of John, verse sixteen: "For God so loved the world that he gave his one and only Son, that whoever believes in him shall not perish but have eternal life." My father spent a lifetime both here and around the world proclaiming this message. His example left a mark on me, especially during a time that turned out to be the crossroads of my professional life.

It happened at the end of a four-month-long trial in 1989 that left me feeling exhausted and defeated. I had put everything into the case, only to see it be dismissed out of hand and without sound reasoning. Words can't explain how frustrated I felt. I really believed I was wasting my time, and so I began asking myself some questions about life:

How do I want to be remembered when I am gone—not gone from the firm, but *gone* gone?

What does it mean to be profitable when God takes a look at the bottom line of my life's contributions?

The more I considered these questions and was honest with myself about the answers, the more I came to realize something: the more success I enjoyed in the practice of law, the less time I had for the things of my heart which had, over the years, become increasingly important to me. Although I soon regained a more positive perspective on my law practice, these stirrings about how I was spending my life wouldn't go away. In fact, they got stronger. I began to wonder whether I was being called to make a dramatic life decision to step out of the practice of law.

Suddenly I was faced with a major decision: If I was going to "follow my heart," how was I going to do it? I didn't want to be seen as abandoning the ship; I was concerned that clients not be disadvantaged or upset by my leaving; I was concerned that I finish strong. A good friend I spoke with gave me some wise advice: "If you find yourself coming back to the same question, then maybe you should do something about it. Don't let the indecision go on for too long."

Almost immediately after receiving that advice, the Canadian Airlines/Air Canada case took me away from home for most of the winter of 1992–93. On returning home in the spring I realized that a large portion of my practice had been farmed out to others and that if I ever intended to "follow my heart," the time was now. The opportunity to step out of my practice "gracefully" had been created by my absence. I tendered my resignation to my partners in these terms:

Many years ago I accepted as true the teachings of the Bible that all of us will spend eternity somewhere and where that will be depends upon what response we make to the claims of Jesus Christ presented in the Bible. The acceptance of that truth has, in recent years, repeatedly raised this question for me: In light of eternity, is my time being spent where it should be spent? The answer to that question has not come easily or quickly, but I have decided that the time has come for me to spend full-time helping to spread the "good news" around the world so that others will know of Jesus Christ and have the opportunity to make their own response.[†]

It was the power of that truth alone that gave rise to my decision.

Rolly's decision to set sail from his law practice and follow God's calling in his life led him to work full-time in Christian world relief ministry. What has his decision to leave port meant? For Rolly it has meant living on a fraction of his former salary, leaving his beautiful new country home near Calgary to reside temporarily in the diesel-fumed chaos of Nairobi, Kenya. It has meant days spent finding creative solutions to a multitude of unique situations that arise in relief work in which there is constantly insufficient time to respond and often inadequate human and other resources readily available. This, coupled with his role as coordinator of the field activities with the head office in the United States, makes life full.

It has also meant setting the alarm for 3:00 A.M., waking up before dawn, then driving fifteen miles to the airport to meet other ministry team members arriving on the 4:30 flight from London. On these mornings, feeling bleary-eyed and tired, the decision to serve others has meant carrying luggage, making all kinds of time-consuming arrangements for others' transportation, lodging, and meals, all the while being tied to a fax machine. Things which he would have had someone do for him in his old firm, Rolly now does himself, willingly and without hesitation. It is just part of the joy that comes as the result of serving others.

Rolly's decision to serve has taken him repeatedly to Rwanda. In the summer of 1994, events in this tiny African country shocked the world as hundreds of thousands of rival Hutu and Tutsi tribespeople were slaughtered and thousands more died of starvation and disease as a result.

Sylvia and I were in Rwanda, just a few miles outside the capital city of Kigali, in June of 1994, while the battle was still raging there. With other members of the relief team from Samaritan's Purse, we had gone to Uganda by small, single-engine aircraft. Then we traveled by truck to a mountaintop refugee camp outside Kigali called Rutare. There we found over 100,000 refugees crowded together, living in small huts made of sticks and leaves and grass. The terrible cost of human hatred was perhaps most evident in the tragedy of nearly four thousand orphaned children who had fled to that mountaintop. About fifteen brave, giving people under the direction of Dr. Paul Jones and his wife, Jan, and Dr. Paul Childs and his wife, Joyce, offered medical care and started an orphanage for these children.

Like Bosnia, Rwanda was part of the new course God had charted for Sylvia and me when we decided to leave the safe harbor of private neurosurgical practice and set out on this new life of service. As in Bosnia, I found God calling our medical team in Rwanda not to tend to the suffering of an entire world but to simply reach out to the needs of one person at a time. As in Bosnia, all that God called me to do in Rwanda was to freely give all that I had and all that I was to that one person, and so it is for each person from Samaritan's Purse who serves there. And in Rwanda, I found that even the threat and sadness of death couldn't rob me of my joy, or cause me to say, "It wasn't worth it."

In the horror of Rwanda I discovered something else, something essential that defines the life of distinction that you and I seek: I found God to be unquestionably real and alive. I witnessed His protection and grace in a forty-six-year-old Rwandan husband and wife I met on our return to their country in December 1994.

When we were on that mountaintop during the time of the fighting in June, I had no idea this couple was only a few miles away and under threat to their lives and those of their children and families. Before I even thought about this chapter, I had no idea that their story, which was yet to happen, would serve as the conclusion for the book. Their nearly three months of constant danger would be the exclamation point of David's message in Psalm 23:

The LORD is my shepherd; I shall not want.
He makes me to lie down in green pastures;
He leads me beside the still waters.
He restores my soul;
He leads me in the paths of righteousness
For His name's sake.

Yea, though I walk through the valley of the shadow of death,
I will fear no evil;
For You are with me;
Your rod and Your staff, they comfort me.

(Psalm 23:1–4)

This is God's promise to you, a promise that He will fulfill as you ask the question, "What will I do with the rest of my life?" The answer is that God will lead you and be with you in all that you do in His service. And as you live into this answer, as you come to the end of yourself and come closer to the heart of God, you can be assured that your life, your decision to serve, is in His hands. As you read the story of the couple I met in Rwanda, you will come to know His faithfulness.

I met Elijah "Elie" Ndaruhutse at the orphanage that Samaritan's Purse had started in Kigali. This tall, thin, and gracious Rwandan man appeared relaxed and happy in a manner that did not even hint of the fears, anguish, and loss which had filled his life over the preceding months. He had accepted Jesus Christ and been baptized when he was twelve. For several years as a young man he worked as a translator at a children's school. But as time went on, Elie felt God calling him to the ministry. He left his work and for four years attended Bible school, then went to Burundi for four more years of seminary. Graduation and marriage were important rites of passage for Elie, but they were dwarfed by the darkening cloud of tribal hatred rumbling in Rwanda.

The nearly seven million people of Rwanda were divided into three tribes—the majority Bahutus (commonly known as Hutus), the minority Batutsi (or Tutsis), and a minute fraction of the population known as the Taws, or Pygmies. For decades the Hutus and Tutsis had fought for power, and their periodic outbreaks had left many thousands dead.

Prior to 1959, Rwanda had been ruled by a Tutsi king. The majority Hutus were bitter; a national election resulted in disputes by the Hutus and continued fighting among the tribes. When Rwanda's Hutu President Habyarimana was killed when his plane was shot down on April 6, 1994, all sense of civil order collapsed. The Hutus took control and went on a killing spree, slaughtering as many as several hundred thousand Tutsis. For the next few days, thousands of Tutsis fled their homes seeking refuge in several large refugee camps. At the same time Elie, his pregnant wife, Judith, and their three children remained in their town of Butare.

One day, the inevitable took place. Elie and his family were at home when Hutu soldiers armed with guns barged into their small house. As they entered the mud-walled hut, they found Elie, Judith, and their children on their knees praying to God for help. Immediately the soldiers ordered the family out of the house while they searched for weapons. Finding none, the soldiers left. Elie wasn't sure what they were mumbling as they fled, but it had to do with why they left, because as best he could hear, they were "afraid to kill godly persons." The words were bittersweet. Even though Elie felt God had protected his family, many other Christians had been killed that day by these Interahamwe—the "Hutus prepared to kill."

"The Interahamwe had guns, machetes, axes, and clubs with sharp nails sticking out of them. These were weapons of killing," Elie told me.

> One night, eight Interahamwe came to our house during the evening. Again, we were inside praying with our children. When the soldiers knocked on our door, my wife said, "Don't open it!" I knew they would blow the door open with a grenade, so I let them in.
>
> Two of the men entered our house. In their hands were machetes. Another six had guns, axes, and clubs. They announced loudly that they had come to kill us because we were Tutsis. They asked me to stand up. Next, they demanded money and took my identification papers. Then, as my heart pounded, they took my wife and children and me out into the darkness. As the men searched our hut, our family continued to pray.
>
> At that moment my wife was so frightened, she became short of breath. Panic set in. The thought of being killed and the feelings of protecting an unborn child were too much for her. The Interahamwe ordered us all back in the house. They wanted to make sure we were inside when they killed us.

Elie stood behind Judith as the soldiers ordered her to her knees. One of the Interahamwe lifted his machete high above her head. He told her she would die first because she was making too much noise trying to breathe.

Then an amazing thing happened, Elie said.

> The arm of the soldier seemed to freeze above my wife's head. He seemed unable to swing the machete downward to

cut her. He got angry, stepped back, and turned to go outside. All the time my wife, my children, and I kept praying out loud to God. The soldier came back in and ordered us to be quiet. But we just kept right on praying.

"We do not kill you tonight," the Interahamwe said, "but we will come again, and *then* we will kill you."

The fear of that threat stayed with Elie and his family for three weeks as they tried to hide in their hut. Then on May fifth, Judith went into labor. She feared having the baby at home unattended, yet she knew that if she left the house and went to the hospital the Hutu soldiers would spot her. They'd know she was a Tutsi and kill her.

But Judith walked to the hospital. In the darkness, in the cold night she reached the guard gate and was surprised to find it unattended. Normally a Hutu guard stood watch. Strangely, on this night, he was gone. She hurried inside the hospital, went down a hall feeling afraid and expectant and gave birth to a baby girl. Then two hours later, she bundled her up and stepped back into the dark night to go back home. Just after passing through the unguarded gate, she heard a sound and turned to see Hutu soldiers return to their post and close the gate. Minutes later she reached the front door of her home, tired, staggering, frightened, and alive.

For several more days the family lived in fear. Then without warning, one night the soldiers came back. This time there were seven. Elie went to the door, opened it and said, "Welcome to our home." Then he calmly sat back down in his chair.

The soldiers fired questions. "Do you have a weapon in your house?"

Elie remained calm. "My only weapon is a weapon

against evil," he answered. "It is my Bible; it is the Word of God." The soldiers weren't satisfied. They blindfolded Elie. He remained seated, as one of the Interahamwe stood behind him. The soldier raised his machete high, to deliver the fatal blow. "Wait a minute before you kill me," Elie said. "I want to talk with you. You are Hutus, but are you good persons? Are all Hutus good persons? If so, you must first determine if I am a bad person before you decide to kill me. Otherwise God will ask you why you killed me. We are not all good persons, but we are not all bad persons just because of the tribe we have been born into. I need to be judged and to be found worthy of death before you kill me."

His words made the soldier frustrated and angry. He carefully lowered the machete from above Elie's head and laid it to the side. He took Elie blindfolded into the other room of the small house, and he and his fellow thugs proceeded to steal his few belongings. One of the men said, "Give us all of your money, and maybe we will not kill you this time."

"I have no money," said Elie.

The soldiers took Elie back into the other room where Judith sat holding their new baby. They asked her about the whereabouts of the other children. "We know you have three children in addition to the baby," they said. "Where are they?" She answered, "When we heard your knock at the door, the three children were so afraid they ran outside. We don't know where they are."

The leader of the Interahamwe group said, "If you're not against us, you must write a statement naming bad things against your tribe and denouncing your people. Otherwise, we'll return and kill you. You must bring your written statement to me tomorrow morning." Then they vanished into the night.

Elie knew exactly what this meant. He knew they were asking him to write his own indictment, his own death sentence. Frustrated, Elie sat down and began to write the words that might spare his life and those of his family. Instead of words of condemnation, all he could write were words of Scripture. First he wrote about the soldiers who had come to arrest Jesus in the Garden of Gethsemane (Matt. 26:47–50).

Then he wrote down what Jesus said when one of those with Him drew a sword and cut off the ear of the slave of the high priest: "Put your sword in its place, for all who take the sword will perish by the sword" (Matt. 26:52).

Elie then recalled Stephen's words from Acts when, having been stoned and near death, he fell on his knees and cried out, "Lord, do not hold this sin against them" (Acts 7:60 NIV). Next, he wrote the familiar words from 2 Chronicles, "If My people who are called by My name will humble themselves, and pray and seek My face, and turn from their wicked ways, then I will hear from heaven, and will forgive their sin and heal their land" (7:14). These words from God's Word would be Elie's rule to live by in his moment of greatest need. He would not try to fight back with a sword. Instead, he would ask God to forgive his enemies. Instead of condemning them, he would humble himself and seek forgiveness for his own wicked ways.

The next morning, having finished writing his testimony, Elie was ready to be killed. He took the paper of the Scripture verses to where the Hutu soldiers had told him. He looked for the Interahamwe, aware that he was being watched. Finally, Elie found the soldiers, found the leader who had wanted his words of self-condemnation. When Elie approached him, the Hutu leader seemed angry, busy, and preoccupied as he took the papers and simply placed them aside. Then he told Elie to go away.

Elie walked home, knowing that somehow the Hutus were through with him. He knew he was no longer going to die, he was going to live. "The Lord didn't want the man to read what I had written," Elie told me. "Otherwise he would have become enraged. He would have killed me on the spot, then marched to my hut and killed my family."

Minutes later, after Elie returned home, he hugged Judith, and the two of them knelt down and thanked the Lord for saving their lives and those of their two daughters. As they prayed they cried twice, out of thankfulness and grief: that morning they had learned that their two sons, ages thirteen and five, had been caught by the Intera- hamwe. When they disappeared out the door of the hut it was the last time Elie and Judith would ever see their two boys. Because they were Tutsis—not because they were a threat, but merely because they were of a different tribe— they were slaughtered.

Two days later the Tutsi-led Rwanda Patriotic Front Army arrived to free Elie's village. From that day forward, Elie and Judith knew they were safe. Safe, yet sobered when they learned that Elie's mother and father, sisters and brothers, and their families—all of Elie's family but one brother—had been killed in this bloody tribal war.

Today, Elie and Judith do not live in despair and grief. "God spared my wife and me and our daughters, and we give Him praise and thanks for this," he said. If I didn't already know the rest of Elie's story, and how he and Judith epitomize a distinctive life of service, I would stop right here and throw up my hands. I would seriously doubt how anyone faced with such grief could respond with such gratitude and keep living with such faith. Like you, there are so many things I don't understand. As a child I was taught the difference between right and wrong. I grew up believing in good and evil. Somehow, as a young person who saw Hitler and Mussolini defeated, I believed that good would eventually triumph over evil on earth. I was even naive enough to believe that such a triumph would happen during my lifetime.

Then I grew up. The spread of drugs, the birth of gangs, the advent of AIDS, and the spread of other diseases like terrorism and apartheid have made me see our world for what it really is: a patient with a very sick heart. For Elie and Judith, this illness proved fatal to their family. Yet in the death of their own sons, they did something remarkable. Instead of remaining dejected or turning their backs on God, they looked for a way they could nurture life.

Today, this couple who lost their only two sons live with happiness on their faces and gratitude in their hearts because they work in an orphanage in Rwanda's capital city of Kigali. Every day they share their lives and their abundant love with more than 460 children who no longer have parents or families of their own, who are part of the nearly one million homeless victims of their country's senseless tribal war. To the government, these boys and girls are known as "unaccompanied minors." To Elie and Judith, they are like their own children. These are children like those you know and love today; children like you and I once were, who run and play and laugh like kids everywhere. These children's memories must contain the vivid images of terror and personal loss of parents and siblings that are far beyond what you or I could ever comprehend. Elie and Judith have placed aside their own memories of terror and loss and have turned their thoughts, their hearts, and their hands to the needs of these children. That is what you call serving others in Jesus' name. That is what you call living a life that counts.

If God can take this humble Rwandan couple away from the brink of death and turn their mourning into giving, what do you think He can do with your life and mine? Not the life you mean to live tomorrow when you plan to sit down and "figure out what I'm doing." Not tomorrow when all the craziness you're feeling at work, with your kids, and with too many commitments begins to ease up. What do you think God can do with your life, with all the indecision and unsettledness you're experiencing *right now*?

Do you know that this anxiety that resides between where you are now and where you want to be can be used for good? Do you know that your life could be forever changed because of what's not clear to you yet—the lack of clear direction, the impatience with God that's been brewing inside you this week as you've been turning the pages of this book?

The very catalyst God can use to change life and make it beyond your wildest dreams is the same thing that brought each of the people in this book to a new beginning. The change agent is no secret. It's not a life truth you can reduce neatly to the size of a refrigerator magnet. The most powerful means available for you or me to know that God is now at work moving us into a life that counts has already been identified:

Consider it pure joy, my brothers, whenever you face trials of many kinds, because you know that the testing of your faith develops perseverance. Perseverance must finish its work so that you may be mature and complete, not lacking anything. (James 1:2–4 NIV)

Today's sermons, devotional booklets, and study guides have caused these words to be so familiar that we neglect to see their real meaning. We neglect to see that they can be a catalyst for turning the present that seems so unresolved into a new purpose and direction for living that can be so right. That catalyst, that change agent that James describes, is the trials that you and I face *right now*, the questions that demand the kind of faith necessary for the kind of life God calls us to live.

The message of James, the message to you and me, is that without doing a thing, without getting up from your seat, you are on the brink of living a new life. This new approach to life is alive in the current unresolved pressures that are causing you to pray, to question, to seek, to obtain the wisdom and direction God is ready to give. You will be tempted to give up. In fact, you may have given up before. But if you choose to walk in the path that the author of James and the rest of God's Word have laid out, you can expect to see footprints up ahead. They were left by people you've already met, men and women who kept following the Carpenter from Nazareth even when they weren't sure where He was leading them.

They are people like Bill James, who repaired broken plumbing because it needed to be fixed and who operated on a person he knew was broke without charge because a life was worth saving.

They are people like Diane Bringgold who, feeling the pain and scars of her terrible burns and the loss of all of her family in a fiery plane crash, knew God wanted her to tell the story of how she almost died to others who had not yet started to live.

And if you feel it's humanly impossible to make sense of what the Bible says about how God wants us to live, you will be as frustrated as Aart Van Wingerden was when he came to that tiny, exasperating sentence in 1 John 3:17, "But whoever has this world's goods, and sees his brother in need, and shuts up his heart from him, how does the love of God abide in him?" Aart's life really began when he read this and said, "*I don't know* how to do this. God, help me, please, to understand."

If your heart has been saying these words out of humble obedience, then you've already begun to live the only kind of life that's really worth living. You've already begun living a life of distinction, a life in which you can truly make a difference. A life that would be humanly impossible to carry out, but that once lived by faith offers meaning and purpose that's impossible to ignore.

Eleanor Roosevelt, who knew something about this new life, said, "When you cease to make a contribution, you begin to die."

Martin Luther King, Jr., knew about this new life when he said, "If a man hasn't discovered something he is willing to die for—he isn't fit to live."

Stephen Greenlet said it a little differently: "I expect to pass through this world but once; any good thing therefore that I can do, or any kindness that I can show to any fellow creature, let me do it now; let me not defer or neglect it, for I shall not pass this way again."

And Fred Rogers, who has welcomed millions of children and adults into his television neighborhood, may not know the journey you're on, but he knows the right question to ask. "It's been said that in his or her lifetime, a person will walk an average of 65,000 miles. That's two and a half times around the earth. How far do you have left to walk? Where will all of your remaining miles take you?"[††]

You and I will have only one chance to answer that question. Like Bob Dennis who prepared to drop food to the starving Dutch families of World War II, you and I will have only one life mission. And like Bob who met one of those recipients fifty years later, you and I can know that our lives counted. We can know that God *does* direct food drops, prayers, and people to their right and perfect destination. On that day when you and I stand before the Lord and answer His question, "What did you do for Me?" we will know what we wanted to believe all along, that one person *can* make a difference and that we can know for certain, "I'm living a life that counts."

Before you turn the page . . .

Before you go to bed tonight, write your "living epitaph." Don't limit yourself to one piece of paper, a crayon, or ten minutes like I did. Take as long as you need to reflect, pray, and then write down your answer to the question, "After I die, how do I want to be remembered? What really counted in my life?"

Think of this statement not as an obituary your friends will read when you die. Think of it as a statement that describes your relationship with God, your gifts, and the unique and special place He's given you to serve. Think of these words not as a memorial to death but as a motivation for life; a personal, daily reminder of how you want to *live today!*

Then, as you live these words this week, this month, this year, you'll be living the answer to the question so many people put off to tomorrow but that you can begin to explore today:

"What will I do with the rest of my life?"

† Gordon MacDonald, *Real World Faith* (Nashville: Thomas Nelson, 1989).

†† Fred Rogers, *You're Special* (New York: Viking Press, 1994), 164.

MELVIN L. CHEATHAM, M.D. is a neurosurgeon who serves as clinical professor of neurosurgery at the University of California (Los Angeles) Medical Center. He is director of the UCLA Microneurosurgery Laboratory and is coeditor of a major neurosurgical textbook, *The Atlas of Cranial Base Surgery*, published by the W. B. Saunders Company.

Dr. Cheatham is author of *Come Walk with Me*, published by Thomas Nelson Publishers. He serves on the Board of Directors for Samaritan's Purse and its medical arm, World Medical Missions. He also serves as director of the West Coast office for these Christian relief organizations. Dr. Cheatham and his wife, Sylvia, travel extensively throughout the world volunteering their time and talents in doing medical work in developing countries and in places of war or other great need. In April 1995, Dr. Cheatham was the recipient of the Humanitarian Award given by the American Association of Neurological Surgeons.

MARK CUTSHALL is a freelance writer who has written for Focus on the Family magazine and has coauthored several books including *Revival Signs: The Coming of Spiritual Awakening*. He also collaborated with Dr. Cheatham on *Come Walk with Me*.

Cutshall has helped numerous people tell their life stories. He is also an accomplished speaker. Mark and his wife, Linda, live in Seattle, Washington, where he heads Mark Cutshall Creative Services.